Miami Marlins 2019

A Baseball Companion

Edited by Patrick Dubuque, Aaron Gleeman and Bret Sayre

Baseball Prospectus

Craig Brown and Dave Pease, Consultant Editors
Rob McQuown and Harry Pavlidis, Statistics Editors

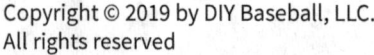

Copyright © 2019 by DIY Baseball, LLC.
All rights reserved

This book or any part thereof may not be reproduced or transmitted in any form or by any means, electronic or mechanical, including photocopying, recording, or by any information storage and retrieval system, without permission in writing from the publisher.

Limit of Liability/Disclaimer of Warranty: While the publisher and the author have used their best efforts in preparing this book, they make no representations or warranties with respect to the accuracy or completeness of the contents of this book and specifically disclaim any implied warranties of merchantability or fitness for a particular purpose. No warranty may be created or extended by sales representatives or written sales materials. The advice and strategies contained herein may not be suitable for your situation. You should consult with a professional where appropriate. Neither the publisher nor the author shall be liable for any loss of profit or any other commercial damages, including but not limited to special, incidental, consequential, or other damages.

Library of Congress Cataloging-in-Publication Data:
paperback
ISBN-13: 978-1-949332-42-1

Project Credits
Cover Design: Kathleen Dyson
Interior Design and Production: Jeff Pease, Dave Pease
Layout: Jeff Pease, Dave Pease

Baseball icon courtesy of Uberux, from https://www.shareicon.net/author/uberux

Ballpark diagram courtesy of Lou Spirito/THIRTY81 Project, https://thirty81project.com/

Manufactured in the United States of America
10 9 8 7 6 5 4 3 2 1

Table of Contents

Foreword v
    Rob Mains

Statistical Introduction vii

Part 1: Team Analysis

Table for Two: Previewing the 2019 Miami Marlins 3
    Nicolas Stellini and Lukas Vlahos

Performance Graphs 9

2018 Team Performance 10

2019 Team Projections 11

Team Personnel 12

Marlins Park Stats 13

Marlins Team Analysis 15

Part 2: Player Analysis

Marlins Player Analysis 22

Marlins Prospects 97

Part 3: Featured Articles

The Hole in The Shift is Fixing Itself 111
    Russell Carleton

The State of the Quality Start 115
    Rob Mains

Heads-Up Hacking—The First Pitch 121
    Matthew Trueblood

A Hymn for the Index Stat 127
    Patrick Dubuque

Index of Names 131

Foreword

Rob Mains

Welcome to this companion of the 2019 Miami Marlins. We at Baseball Prospectus are excited to provide this analysis of the Marlins.

Our website, Baseball Prospectus, is a leader in delivering high-quality commentary and data to baseball fans everywhere. To some, those words—commentary and data—appear mutually exclusive. There are people out there who believe that traditional analysis and advanced analytics must run on different paths. But the simplistic narrative of stats vs. traditionalists just isn't true. Every team's analytics department interacts with scouting, development, and major league operations with a common goal: Delivering a championship. New technologies, like radar tracking of pitch speeds and movement, enable talent evaluators to focus on qualitative aspects of pitching like mechanics and pitch sequencing. In-game strategies like infield shifts, based on batters' hit tendencies, help turn balls in play into outs. Hitters use information to adjust their swings to maximize run production.

All these numbers can seem, at best, intimidating, and at worst, counterproductive to the casual fan. Even as technology and analysis have embedded themselves deeply into the way teams run, it can often feel like statistics create a displacement between the viewer and the sport, breaking them out of the action. And yet every fan incorporates the numbers to some degree; stats like batting average and earned run average, so fundamental to how we talk about performance, are actually complicated formulas. They don't bother people because those formulas have become second nature, as easy to translate as the action on the field.

Along the way, new statistics have entered baseball's lexicon. You'll see some of them, like on-base percentage (which measures a batter's ability to get on base via walk, hit batter, or hit), OPS (on-base plus slugging), and average exit velocity (the speed of balls off a hitter's bat) on broadcasts. Others, like DRC+, might well be new to you. Some of them have been well-defined to the public, others haven't. That lack of context has created ambiguity. Fans know that a ball hit 100 mph is scorched, but does that mean extra bases? (Not if it's hit on the ground or high in the air it doesn't.)

For those who are amenable to them, the new statistics can increase the enjoyment and understanding of the game. They can help fans identify when a pitcher is tiring, when a stolen base or a bunt attempt makes sense (and, more often, when it doesn't), or how a team's lineup might be constructed. Websites like Baseball Prospectus add to that understanding by weaving metrics into the narrative of the game. That's the goal of this publication: to take some of the newer, more complicated statistics and make them as intuitive as the ones on the back of old baseball cards.

But you don't need to love analytics to love baseball. The fans at BP who worked together to write this guide are captivated first and foremost by the game itself. We're drawn to Aaron Judge's power, Francisco Lindor's glove, Billy Hamilton's speed and Patrick Corbin's slider and don't need numbers to tell us why they're so mesmerizing. The underlying statistics provide depth to the game that we all love.

We hope you'll find that this guide helps you better understand the Marlins. Our analysts have studied the team's major league personnel and its minor league affiliates to identify their strengths and weaknesses, both the obvious ones and those that only a careful dissection of players' performances—yes, including the data—can reveal. You don't need us to tell you who was good and who wasn't in 2018, but our models and writers can help you project how each player is going to perform this year and beyond, and appreciate the greatness of each new game as it unfolds. As in the sport itself, the human and analytic components combine to generate a deeper overall understanding.

Think back to the first time you saw a baseball game on a high-definition TV. You'd grown familiar with how the game looked and felt on a picture tube. But new TV allowed you to see details that you'd never seen before. That's how advanced statistics work. The game itself is why you're here and why you're buying this. (And, for that matter, why we wrote it.) The statistical measures provide the sharper focus, the detail, the depth of knowledge that you didn't have before, generating an overall superior picture. Enjoy the view.

—*Rob Mains is an author of Baseball Prospectus.*

Statistical Introduction

Sports are, fundamentally, a blend of athletic endeavor and storytelling. Baseball, like any other sport, tells its stories in so many ways: in the arc of a game from the stands or a season from the box scores, in photos, or even in numbers. At Baseball Prospectus, we understand that statistics don't replace observation or any of baseball's stories, but complement everything else that makes the game so much fun.

What stats help us with is with patterns and precision, variance and value. This book can help you learn things you may not see from watching a game or hundred, whether it's the path of a career over time or the breadth of the entire MLB. We'd also never ask you to choose between our numbers and the experience of viewing a game from the cheap seats or the comfort of your home; our publication combines running the numbers with observations and wisdom from some of the brightest minds we can find. But if you *do* want to learn more about the numbers beyond what's on the backs of player jerseys, let us help explain.

Offense

At the end of this past year, we've revised our methodology for determining batting value. Long-time readers of Baseball Prospectus will notice that we've retired True Average in favor of a new metric: Deserved Runs Created Plus (DRC+). Developed by Jonathan Judge and our stats team, this statistic measures everything a player does at the plate–reaching base, hitting for power, making outs, and moving runners over–and puts it on a scale where 100 equals league-average performance. A DRC+ of 150 is terrific, a DRC+ of 100 is average, and a DRC+ of 75 means you better be an excellent defender.

DRC+ also does a better job than any of our previous metrics in taking contextual factors into account. The model adjusts for how the park affects performance, but also for things like the talent of the opposing pitcher, value of different types of batted-ball events, league, temperature, and other factors. It's able to describe a player's expected offensive contribution than any other statistic we've found over the years, and also does a better job of predicting future performance as well.

Miami Marlins 2019

The other aspect of run-scoring is baserunning, which we quantify using Baserunning Runs. BRR not only records the value of stolen bases (or getting caught in the act), but also accounts for a runner's ability to go first to third on a single or advance on a fly ball.

Defense

Where offensive value is *relatively* easy to identify and understand, defensive value is ... not. Over the past dozen years, the sabermetric community has focused mostly on stats based on zone data: a real-live human person records the type of batted ball and estimated landing location, and models are created that give expected outs. From there, you can compare fielders' actual outs to those expected ones. Simple, right?

Unfortunately, zone data has two major issues. First, zone data is recorded by commercial data providers who keep the raw data private unless you pay for it. (All the statistics we build in this book and on our website use public data as inputs.) That hurts our ability to test assumptions or duplicate results. Second, over the years it has become apparent that there's quite a bit of "noise" in zone-based fielding analysis. Sometimes the conclusions drawn from zone data don't hold up to scrutiny, and sometimes the different data provided by different providers don't look anything alike, giving wildly different results. Sometimes the hard-working professional stringers or scorers might unknowingly inflict unconscious bias into the mix: for example good fielders will often be credited with more expected outs despite the data, and ballparks with high press boxes tend to score more line drives than ones with a lower press box.

Enter our Fielding Runs Above Average (FRAA). For most positions, FRAA is built from play-by-play data, which allows us to avoid the subjectivity found in many other fielding metrics. The idea is this: count how many fielding plays are made by a given player and compare that to expected plays for an average fielder at their position (based on pitcher ground-ball tendencies and batter handedness). Then we adjust for park and base-out situations.

When it comes to catchers, our methodology is a little different thanks to the laundry list of responsibilities they're tasked with beyond just, well, catching and throwing the ball. By now you've probably heard about "framing" or the art of making umpires more likely to call balls outside the strike zone for strikes. To put this into one tidy number, we incorporate pitch tracking data (for the years it exists) and adjust for important factors like pitcher, umpire, batter, and home-field advantage using a mixed-model approach. This grants us a number for how many strikes the catcher is personally adding to (or subtracting from) his pitchers' performance ... which we then convert to runs added or lost using linear weights.

Framing is one of the biggest parts of determining catcher value, but we also take into account blocking balls from going past, whether a scorer deems it a passed ball or a wild pitch. We use a similar approach–one that really benefits from the pitch tracking data that tells us what ends up in the dirt and what doesn't. We also include a catcher's ability to prevent stolen bases and how well they field balls in play, and *finally* we come up with our FRAA for catchers.

Pitching

Both pitching and fielding make up the half of baseball that isn't run scoring: run prevention. Separating pitching from fielding is a tough task, and most recent pitching analysis has branched off from Voros McCracken's famous (and controversial) statement, "There is little if any difference among major-league pitchers in their ability to prevent hits on balls hit in the field of play." The research of the analytic community has validated this to some extent, and there are a host of "defense-independent" pitching measures that have been developed to try and extricate the effect of the defense behind a hurler from the pitcher's work.

Our solution to this quandry is Deserved Run Average (DRA), our core pitching metric. DRA looks like earned run average (ERA), the tried-and-true pitching stat you've seen on every baseball broadcast or box score from the past century, but it's very different. To start, DRA takes an event-by-event look at what the pitchers does, and adjusts the value of that event based on different environmental factors like park, batter, catcher, umpire, base-out situation, run differential, inning, defense, home field advantage, pitcher role, and temperature. That mixed model gives us a pitcher's expected contribution, similar to what we do for our DRC+ model for hitters and FRAA model for catchers. (Oh, and we also consider the pitcher's effect on basestealing and on balls getting past the catcher.)

It's important to note that DRA is set to the scale of runs allowed per nine innings (RA9) instead of ERA, which makes DRA's scale slightly higher than ERA's. The reason for this is because ERA tends to overrate three types of pitchers:

1. Pitchers who play in parks where scorers hand out more errors. Official scorers differ significantly in the frequency at which they assign errors to fielders.
2. Ground-ball pitchers, because a substantial proportion of errors occur on grounders.
3. Pitchers who aren't very good. Better pitchers often allow fewer unearned runs than bad pitchers, because good pitchers tend to find ways to get out of jams.

Since the last time you picked up an edition of this book, we've also made a few minor changes to DRA to make it better. Recent research into "tunneling"–the act of throwing consecutive pitches that appear similar from a batter's point of view until after the swing decision point–data has given us a new contextual factor to account for in DRA: plate distance. This refers to the distance between successive pitches as they approach the plate, and while it has a smaller effect than factors like velocity or whiff rate, it still can help explain pitcher strikeout rate in our model.

New Pitching Metrics for 2019

We're including a few "new" pitching metrics for 2019's suite of Baseball Prospectus publications, but you may be familiar with them if you've spent time scouring the internet for stats.

Fastball Percentage

Our fastball percentage (FB%) statistic measures how frequently a pitcher throws a pitch classified as a "fastball," measured as a percentage of overall pitches thrown. We qualify three types of fastballs:

1. The traditional four-seam fastball;
2. The two-seam fastball or sinker;
3. "Hard cutters," which are pitches that have the movement profile of a cut fastball and are used as the pitcher's primary offering or in place of a more traditional fastball.

For example, a pitcher with a FB% of 67 throws any combination of these three pitches about two-thirds of the time.

Whiff Rate

Everybody loves a swing and a miss, and whiff rate (WHF) measures how frequently pitchers induce a swinging strike. To calculate WHF, we add up all the pitches thrown that ended with a swinging strike, then divide that number by a pitcher's total pitches thrown. Most often, high whiff rates correlate with high strikeout rates (and overall effective pitcher performance).

Called Strike Probability

Called Strike Probability (CSP) is a number that represents the likelihood that all of a pitcher's pitches will be called a strike while controlling for location, pitcher and batter handedness, umpire and count. Here's how it works: on each pitch, our model determines how many times (out of 100) that a similar pitch was called for a strike given those factors mentioned above, and when normalized for each batter's strike zone. Then we average the CSP for all pitches thrown by a pitcher in a season, and that gives us the yearly CSP percentage you see in the stats boxes.

As you might imagine, pitchers with a higher CSP are more likely to work in the zone, where pitchers with a lower CSP are likely locating their pitches outside the normal strike zone, for better or for worse.

Projections

Many of you aren't turning to this book just for a look at what a player has done, but for a look at what a player is going to do: the PECOTA projections. PECOTA, initially developed by Nate Silver (who has moved on to greater fame as a political analyst), consists of three parts:

1. Major-league equivalencies, which use minor-league statistics to project how a player will perform in the major leagues;
2. Baseline forecasts, which use weighted averages and regression to the mean to estimate a player's current true talent level; and
3. Aging curves, which uses the career paths of comparable players to estimate how a player's statistics are likely to change over time.

With all those important things covered, let's take a look at what's in the book this year.

Team Prospectus

You bought this book to learn more about your favorite (or maybe least-favorite, who are we to judge?) team, so let's talk about them. After a thoughtful preview of the 2019 season, you'll be presented with our Team Prospectus. This outlines many of the key statistics for each team's 2018 season, as well as a very inviting stadium diagram.

First you'll find the Performance Graphs page. The first is the 2018 Hit List Ranking. This shows our Hit List Rank for the team on each day of the 2018 season and is intended to give you a picture of the ups and downs of the team's season, including their highest and lowest ranks of the year. Hit List Rank measures overall team performance and drives the Hit List Power Rankings at the baseballprospectus.com website.

The second graph is Committed Payroll and helps you see how the team's payroll has compared to the MLB and divisional average payrolls over time. Payroll figures are currents as of January 1, 2019; with so many free agents still unsigned as of this writing, the final 2018 figure will likely be significantly different for many teams. (In the meantime, you can always find the most current data at Baseball Prospectus' Cot's Baseball Contracts page.)

Miami Marlins 2019

The third graph is Farm System Ranking and displays how the Baseball Prospectus prospect team has ranked the organization's farm system since 2007. It also indicates the highest and lowest ranks that the farm system achieved over that time.

We start the Team Performance page with the squad's unadjusted and third-order 2018 win-loss records, presented in divisional context. We then list the three highest performing hitters and pitchers by WARP for 2018. Beneath that are a host of other team statistics. **Pythag** presents an adjusted 2018 winning percentage, calculated by taking runs scored per game (**RS/G**) and runs allowed per game (**RA/G**) for the team, and running them through a version of Bill James' Pythagorean formula that was refined and improved by David Smyth and Brandon Heipp. (The formula is called "Pythagenpat," which is equally fun to type and to say.)

Next up is **DRC+**, described earlier, to indicate the overall hitting ability of the team either above or below league-average. Run prevention on the pitching side is covered by **DRA** (also mentioned earlier) and another metric: Fielding Independent Pitching (**FIP**), which calculates another ERA-like statistic based on strikeouts, walks, and home runs recorded. Defensive Efficiency Rating (**DER**) tells us the percentage of balls in play turned into outs for the team, and is a quick fielding shorthand that rounds out run prevention.

After that, we have several measures related to roster composition, as opposed to on-field performance. **B-Age** and **P-Age** tell us the average age of a team's batters and pitchers, respectively. **Salary** is the combined team payroll for all on-field players, and Doug Pappas' Marginal Dollars per Marginal Win (**M$/MW**) tells us how much money a team spent to earn production above replacement level.

Ending this batch of statistics is the number of disabled list days a team had over the season (**DL Days**) and the amount of salary paid to players on the disabled list (**$ on DL**); this final number is expressed as a percentage of total payroll.

Next to each of these stats, we've listed each team's MLB rank in that category from 1st to 30th. In this, 1st always indicates a positive outcome and 30th a negative outcome, except in the case of salary–1st is highest.

The Team Projections page is intended to convey the team's operational capacity entering the 2019 season. We start with the team's PECOTA projected record for 2019, again in divisional context. The **+/-** column indicates how many more or less wins the team is projected to get than they got in 2018. We then list the three highest projected hitters and pitchers by WARP for 2018. A brief farm system summary follows, with the team's top prospect and number of BP Top 101 Prospects. Finally, we list the key new players and departed players, along with their 2019 projected WARP.

Alex Bregman 3B

Born: 03/30/94   Age: 25   Bats: R   Throws: R
Height: 6'0"   Weight: 180   Origin: Round 1, 2015 Draft (#2 overall)

YEAR	TEAM	LVL	AGE	PA	R	2B	3B	HR	RBI	BB	K	SB	CS	AVG/OBP/SLG
2016	CCH	AA	22	285	54	16	2	14	46	42	26	5	3	.297/.415/.559
2016	FRE	AAA	22	83	17	6	0	6	15	5	12	2	1	.333/.373/.641
2016	HOU	MLB	22	217	31	13	3	8	34	15	52	2	0	.264/.313/.478
2017	HOU	MLB	23	626	88	39	5	19	71	55	97	17	5	.284/.352/.475
2018	HOU	MLB	24	705	105	51	1	31	103	96	85	10	4	.286/.394/.532
2019	HOU	MLB	25	675	96	38	3	23	78	73	107	12	4	.272/.359/.463

Breakout: 6%   Improve: 52%   Collapse: 5%   Attrition: 2%   MLB: 100%
Comparables: Anthony Rendon, David Wright, Pablo Sandoval

YEAR	TEAM	LVL	AGE	PA	DRC+	VORP	BABIP	BRR	FRAA	WARP
2016	CCH	AA	22	285	172	38.9	.286	1.6	SS(51): -3.4, 3B(11): 1.4	2.7
2016	FRE	AAA	22	83	161	10.0	.333	-1.2	SS(14): 2.1, LF(3): -0.1	0.8
2016	HOU	MLB	22	217	107	9.6	.317	0.5	3B(40): 0.9, SS(6): -0.1	1.1
2017	HOU	MLB	23	626	114	34.7	.311	-1.5	3B(132): 8.7, SS(30): -2.9	3.9
2018	HOU	MLB	24	705	150	72.6	.289	-1.6	3B(136): 5.4, SS(28): -0.4	7.4
2019	HOU	MLB	25	675	125	37.3	.295	0.0	3B 7, SS 0	4.6

After the projections page, we share a few items about the team's home ballpark. There's the aforementioned diagram of the park's dimensions (including distances to the outfield wall), a few important biographical facts about the stadium, a graphic showing the height of the wall from the left-field pole to the right-field pole, and a table showing three-year park factors for the stadium. The park factors are displayed as indexes where 100 is average, 110 means that the park inflates the statistic in question by 10 percent, and 90 means that the park deflates the statistic in question by 10 percent.

Following the ballpark page, we have a **Personnel** section that lists many of the important decision-makers and upper-level field and operations staff members for the franchise, as well as any former Baseball Prospectus staff members who are currently part of the organization.

Position Players

After all that information and a thoughtful bylined essay covering each team, we present our player comments. Each player is listed with the major-league team who employed him as of early January 2019. If a player changed teams after that point via free agency, trade, or any other method, you'll be able to find them in the book for their previous squad.

First, we cover biographical information (age is as of June 30, 2019) before moving onto the stats themselves. Our statistic columns include standard identifying information like **YEAR**, **TEAM**, **LVL** (level of affiliated play) and **AGE** before getting into the numbers. Next, we provide raw, unstranslated numbers like you might find on the back of your dad's baseball cards: **PA** (plate appearances), **R** (runs), **2B** (doubles), **3B** (triples), **HR** (home runs), **RBI** (runs batted in), **BB** (walks), **K** (strikeouts), **SB** (stolen bases) and **CS** (caught stealing). Then we have unadjusted "slash" statistics: **AVG** (batting average), **OBP** (on-base percentage) and **SLG** (slugging percentage).

Just below the stats box is **PECOTA** data, which is discussed further in a following section. After that, it's on to a pithy and always-informative comment written by a member of the Baseball Prospectus staff, before we cover more stats.

The second text box repeats YEAR, TEAM, LVL, AGE, and PA, then moves on to **DRC+** (Deserved Runs Created Plus), which we described earlier as total offensive expected contribution compared to the league average. Next, one of our oldest active metrics, **VORP** (Value Over Replacement Player), considers offensive production, position and plate appearances. In essence, it is the number of runs contributed beyond what a replacement-level player at the same position would contribute if given the same percentage of team plate appearances. VORP does not consider the quality of a player's defense.

BABIP (batting average on balls in play) tells us how often a ball in play fell for a hit, and can help us identify whether a batter may have been lucky or not ... but note that high BABIPs also tend to follow the great hitters of our time, as well as speedy singles hitters who put the ball on the ground.

The next item is **BRR** (Baserunning Runs), which covers all of a player's baserunning accomplishments which includes (but isn't limited to) swiped bags and failed attempts. Next is **FRAA** (Fielding Runs Above Average), which also includes the number of games previously played at each position noted in parentheses. Multi-position players have only their two most frequent positions listed here, but their total FRAA number reflects all positions played.

Our last column here is **WARP** (Wins Above Replacement Player). WARP estimates the total value of a player, which means for hitters it takes into account hitting runs above average (calculated using the DRC+ model), BRR and FRAA. Then, it makes an adjustment for positions played and gives the player a credit for plate appearances based upon the difference between "replacement level"¬–which is derived from the quality of players added to a team's roster after the start of the season¬–and the league average.

Catchers

Catchers are a special breed, and thus they have earned their own separate box which displays some of the defensive metrics that we've built just for them. As an example, let's check out J.T. Realmuto.

YEAR	TEAM	P. COUNT	FRM RUNS	BLK RUNS	THRW RUNS	TOT RUNS
2016	MIA	18935	-8.5	1.8	2.1	-5.6
2017	MIA	18959	5.3	1.7	1.0	9.1
2018	MIA	16399	-0.4	0.9	0.1	0.4
2019	PHI	18448	-1.4	1.5	0.7	0.8

The **YEAR** and **TEAM** columns match what you'd find in the other stat box. **P. COUNT** indicates the number of pitches thrown while the catcher was behind the plate, including swinging strikes, fouls, and balls in play. **FRM RUNS** is the total run value the catcher provided (or cost) his team by influencing the umpire to call strikes where other catchers did not. **BLK RUNS** expresses the total run value above or below average for the catcher's ability to prevent wild pitches and passed balls. **THRW RUNS** is calculated using a similar model as the previous two statistics, and it measures a catcher's ability to throw out basestealers but also to dissuade them from testing his arm in the first place. It takes into account factors like the pitcher (including his delivery and pickoff move) and baserunner (who could be as fast as Billy Hamilton or as slow as Yonder Alonso). **TOT RUNS** is the sum of all of the previous three statistics.

Pitchers

Let's give our pitchers a turn, using 2018 NL Cy Young winner Jacob deGrom as our example. Take a look at his first stat block: the first line and the **YEAR**, **TEAM**, **LVL** and **AGE** columns are the same as in the position player example earlier.

Here too, we have a series of columns that display raw, unadjusted statistics compiled by the pitcher over the course of a season: **W** (wins), **L** (losses), **SV** (saves), **G** (games pitched), **GS** (games started), **IP** (innings pitched), **H** (hits allowed) and **HR** (home runs allowed). Next we have two statistics that are rates: **BB/9** (walks per nine innings) and **K/9** (strikeouts per nine innings), before returning to the unadjusted **K** (strikeouts).

Next up is **GB%** (ground ball percentage), which is the percentage of all batted balls that were hit in the ground, including both outs and hits. Remember, this is based on observational data and subject to human error, so please approach this with a healthy dose of skepticism.

BABIP (batting average on balls in play) is calculated using the same methodology as it is for position players, but it often tells us more about a pitcher than it does a hitter. With pitchers, a high BABIP is often due to poor defense or bad luck, and can often be an indicator of potential rebound, and a low BABIP may be cause to expect performance regression. (A typical league-average BABIP is close to .290-.300.)

After a witty 150ish words on the player like only Baseball Prospectus's staff can provide, it's on to that second stat block, which repeats the YEAR, TEAM, LVL, and AGE columns. The metrics **WHIP** (walks plus hits per inning pitched) and **ERA**

Miami Marlins 2019

(earned run average) are old standbys: WHIP measures walks and hits allowed on a per-inning basis, while ERA measures earned runs on a nine-inning basis. Neither of these stats are translated or adjusted.

DRA (Deserved Run Average) was described at length earlier, and measures how many runs the pitcher "deserved" to allow per nine innings. Please note that since we lack all the data points that would make for a "real" DRA for minor-league events, the DRA displayed for minor league partial-seasons is based off of different data. (That data is a modified version of our cFIP metric, which you can find more information about on our website.)

Jacob deGrom   RHP
Born: 06/19/88   Age: 31   Bats: L   Throws: R
Height: 6'4"   Weight: 180   Origin: Round 9, 2010 Draft (#272 overall)

YEAR	TEAM	LVL	AGE	W	L	SV	G	GS	IP	H	HR	BB/9	K/9	K	GB%	BABIP
2016	NYN	MLB	28	7	8	0	24	24	148	142	15	2.2	8.7	143	47%	.312
2017	NYN	MLB	29	15	10	0	31	31	201[1]	180	28	2.6	10.7	239	48%	.305
2018	NYN	MLB	30	10	9	0	32	32	217	152	10	1.9	11.2	269	48%	.281
2019	NYN	MLB	31	13	9	0	31	31	186	145	18	2.3	10.7	221	46%	.286

Breakout: 8%   Improve: 29%   Collapse: 28%   Attrition: 6%   MLB: 85%
Comparables: Erik Bedard, A.J. Burnett, CC Sabathia

YEAR	TEAM	LVL	AGE	WHIP	ERA	DRA	WARP	MPH	FB%	WHF	CSP
2016	NYN	MLB	28	1.20	3.04	3.30	3.5	96.3	59.6	12.1	47.2
2017	NYN	MLB	29	1.19	3.53	3.02	5.7	97.2	55.5	14.5	49.5
2018	NYN	MLB	30	0.91	1.70	2.09	8.0	98.2	52.1	16.3	48.4
2019	NYN	MLB	31	1.02	2.91	3.23	3.9	96.6	54.5	14.8	48.2

Just like with hitters, **WARP** (Wins Above Replacement Player) is a total value metric that puts pitchers of all stripes on the same scale as position players. We use DRA as the primary input for our calculation of WARP. You might notice that relief pitchers (due to their limited innings) may have a lower WARP than you were expecting or than you might see in other WARP-like metrics. WARP does not take leverage into account, just the actions a pitcher performs and the expected value of those actions ... which ends up judging high-leverage relief pitchers differently than you might imagine given their prestige and market value.

MPH gives you the pitcher's 95th percentile velocity for the noted season, in order to give you an idea of what the *peak* fastball velocity a pitcher possesses. Since this comes from our pitch tracking data, it is not publicly available for minor-league pitchers.

Finally, we display the three new pitching metrics we described earlier. **FB%** (fastball percentage) gives you the percentage of fastballs thrown out of all pitches. **WhiffRt** (whiff rate) tells you the percentage of swinging strikes induced out of all pitches. **CS Prob** (called strike probability) expresses the likelihood of all pitches thrown to result in a called strike, after controlling for factors like handedness, umpire, pitch type, count, and location.

PECOTA

All players have PECOTA projections for 2019, as well as a set of other numbers that describe the performance of comparable players according to PECOTA. All projections for 2019 are for the player at the date we went to press in early January and are projected into the league and park context as indicated by the team abbreviation. All PECOTA projected statistics represent a player's projected major-league performance.

The numbers beneath the player's stats–Breakout, Improve, Collapse, Attrition–are part and parcel of the PECOTA projections. They estimate the likelihood of changes in performance relative to the player's previously-established level of production, based on the performance of comparable players:

Breakout Rate is the percent change that a player's production will improve by at least 20 percent relative to the weighted average of his performance over his most recent seasons.

Improve Rate is the percent chance that a player's production will improve at all relative to his baseline performance. A player who is expected to perform just the same as he has in the recent past will have an Improve Rate of 50 percent.

Collapse Rate is the percent chance that a position player's production will decline by at least 25 percent relative to his baseline performance.

Attrition Rate operates on playing time rather than performance. Specifically, it measures the likelihood that a player's playing time will decrease by at least 50 percent relative to his established level.

Breakout Rate and Collapse Rate can sometimes be counterintuitive for players who have already experienced a radical change in performance level. It's also worth noting that the projected decline in a player's rate performances might not be indicative of an expected decline in underlying ability or skill, but could just be an anticipated correction following a breakout season.

MLB% is the percentage of similar players who played in the major leagues in their relevant season.

The final pieces of information are the player's three highest-scoring comparable players as determined by PECOTA. All comparables represent a snapshot of how the listed player was performing at the same age as the current player, so if a 23-year-old pitcher is compared to Bartolo Colon, he's actually being compared to a 23-year-old Colon, not the version that pitched for the Rangers in 2018, nor to Colon's career as a whole.

Miami Marlins 2019

A few points about pitcher projections. First, we aren't yet projecting peak velocity, so that column will be blank in the PECOTA lines. Second, projecting DRA is trickier than evaluating past performance, because it is unclear how deserving each pitcher will be of his anticipated outcomes. However, we know that another DRA-related statistic–contextual FIP or cFIP–estimates future run scoring very well. So for PECOTA, the projected DRA figures you see are based on the past cFIPs generated by the pitcher and comparable players over time, along with the other factors described above.

Lineouts

In each chapter's Lineouts section, you'll find abbreviated text comments, as well as most of same information you'd find in our full player comments. We limit the stats boxes in this section to only including the 2018 information for each player.

Exclusive Player Visualizations

In our constant battle to provide you with new and interesting baseball content you can't find anywhere else, we've added a trio of data visualizations to each hitter's entry in these books and a pair of visualizations for each pitcher.

For hitters, you'll find three new infographics. The first is each player's **Batted Ball Distribution**, which displays the five major sections of the field: LF (left), LCF (left center), CF (center), RCF (right center), and RF (right). The percentage indicated tells us what percentage of batted balls from that hitter fell within that part of the field during the 2018 season. We've also included the hitter's slugging percentage on balls in play (also called **SLGCON**) for that part of the field.

You'll also see two heatmaps: **Strike Zone vs LHP** and **Strike Zone vs RHP**. These heat maps represent a view of the strike zone from behind the catcher. Areas where there is a darker coloration represent the places where a higher percentage of pitches resulted in hits. In other words, the heatmap represents a hitter's "sweet spots" for getting hits against either left-handed or right-handed pitchers, depending on the image.

Pitchers get two images that help explain what their pitches look like from a hitter's perspective: **Pitch Shape vs LHH** and **Pitch Shape vs RHH**. These images show you the shape and the "tunneling" effect of each pitcher's offerings from the batter's perspective. For each type of pitch that a pitcher throws (represented by an indicator shape), there's a set of dots indicating the flight path, where each dot represents a 0.01-second interval. This maps the average trajectory and speed of an offering, ending where the ball crosses the plate. The solid black box represents the regular strike zone, while the gray contour lines indicate the range of locations that a pitcher typically works in.

Below the image, we provide a bit more detailed information about each pitcher's average offering in the **Pitch Types** box. Here, we also list each of the pitcher's major offerings under the **Type** column.

- **Fastballs** (which usually refers to the four-seam variation)
- **Sinkers** and/or two-seam fastballs
- **Cutters** (which could include "hard" cutters like cut fastballs and "soft" cutters that resemble hard sliders)
- **Changeups** (not including most splitters)
- **Splitters** (split-fingered pitches, forkballs, and some split-changes)
- **Sliders** and/or slurves
- **Curveballs** (including spike-curveballs and knuckle-curveballs, as well as some slurvy curves)
- **Slow curveballs** and/or eephus pitches
- **Knuckleballs**
- **Screwballs**

The **Freq** column indicates the percentage of overall pitches that fall into each of those type categories; if a pitcher has a 16.55% score for changeups, then that's the percent of all pitches that he throws as changeups. **Velo** is exactly what you think it is: the average miles per hour for each pitch type. **H Mov** is the number of inches of horizontal movement on the average pitch of that type, while **V Mov** is the number of inches of vertical movement on the average pitch of that type. (At Baseball Prospectus, we measure this over the long flight of the ball and include gravity into the V Mov number in order to give you the most realistic representation of what the pitch *actually* does.)

If you're wondering about the second number in brackets, that's the index for that velocity or movement compared to the league average. Like DRC+, a score of 100 means that the speed or movement is about the same as league average, while a higher score means that there's higher velocity or movement than the league average. Numbers below 100 indicate less velocity or movement than the league average.

Part 1: Team Analysis

Table for Two: Previewing the 2019 Miami Marlins

Nicolas Stellini and Lukas Vlahos

LUKAS VLAHOS: Let's not bury the lede here: The Marlins are bad. Their roster would be the worst in baseball if the Orioles didn't exist. They took an exciting young core that included the last two NL MVPs and the best catcher in baseball and turned it into a catcher who can't hit, a CF who can't hit, some middling hitting prospects, and a high-risk, high-reward pitching prospect our prospect team loves, but who also has a huge delta in terms of possible outcomes. The farm is still mediocre at best, and PECOTA projects that the Marlins will lose a whopping 94 games.

Meanwhile, Derek Jeter is 'impatient' about winning. The Marlins have a $61 million payroll heading into 2019 (third lowest in baseball), were at $92 million in 2018 (fifth lowest in baseball), and haven't given a free agent more than $2 million (Neil Walker) since Jeter took over, but the CEO says the team has an 'opportunity to win'. It seems Jeter is more impatient about getting whatever money he can off the books to pay down some of the debt used to purchase the team, but hey, what do we really know.

We'll try to talk about some reasons to get excited about the 2019 Marlins, but this is really an exercise in making lemonade out of some extremely low-quality, semi-rotten lemons.

NICK STELLINI: So there's some... interesting components on this team, I think. The Marlins are going to be bad, yes. And they're going to be bad for years to come. The payroll is spare change Jeter found in his couch.

I think I'm on the record as being a Jorge Alfaro Guy. If I wasn't, I am now. He crushed it on defense last year (12.2 FRAA!) and even though he was on top prospect lists for something like half a century, he's still just entering his age-26 season. I still think there's a chance he can hit. He reduced his elephantine strikeout rate as the season went along and catchers, as Jeffrey and Jarrett are fond of saying, are weird. Even if he's just baseball's version of a 3-and-D player, that's a pretty good outcome behind the plate. Now, he *is* going to be playing half his games in Miami, so that power tool may be dampened if he can really start getting it into games.

Miami Marlins 2019

There's also, uhhh… well, Trevor Richards emerged from the ether with one of the best changeups in baseball, so that's fun. Pablo Lopez might be a fungible control artist fifth starter. Brian Anderson can hit. Uhhhhh…

Oh, here's something. PECOTA thinks Lewis Brinson is going to turn in a nearly 2-WARP season. That's not exactly a breakout, but it's a big improvement from one of the more disappointing rookie seasons last year. Brinson's still got a boatload of talent and a 94 DRC+ would certainly be a more welcome sight than last year's 64.

LUKAS: I'm not surprised that he's projected to improve, simply because it'd be nearly impossible for Brinson to be worse. To be fair, he was a guy who routinely had some extremely ugly initial struggles after promotions, then slowly adjusted, and he eventually posted monster numbers at every level of the minors. Still, I'm skeptical of PECOTA's projection here for a guy with such major contact and pitch recognition issues. I also find it a bit odd that he's projected for a significantly better average but fewer home runs—if Brinson figures out how to raise his average 50 points, I expect the power to be there too.

On the pitching side, I think the Marlins pitcher to watch is Caleb Smith. He came firing out of the gate last year, racking up 69 strikeouts in 56 innings before a lat injury led to a rough June and eventual surgery. His slider is a really good pitch that batters can't seem to square up. He was never a guy who was heralded as a top prospect, and he's been slowed down a lot by injury, but he's one of the few legitimately good pieces on this team. If he's healthy, I think we'll see him breakout well past the 0.5 WARP PECOTA pegs him for.

NICK: Teams generally need to have those sorts of unexpected breakouts as they work their way back from the rebuilding abyss. It helps when you can turn some of those assets into useful players. The Marlins are definitely hoping to that given what they've gotten back for their All-Stars in all those trades. Sure, Sixto Sanchez, Sandy Alcantara, Monte Harrison and Isan Diaz are nice to have. They're not exactly the backbone of a powerhouse farm system.

On top of that, the Marlins are nearly out of tradable assets. Drew Steckenrider, Starlin Castro, Dan Straily and Sergio Romo are all candidates to be moved this summer, among others. None of them are likely going to fetch anything worth writing home about. It'll be depth that Miami doesn't currently have right now, but it's not going to move the needle a ton.

It'll help them pick near the top of the draft again, that's for sure. And it'll help them get more talent to put in the system alongside those guys and Victor Victor Mesa, one of the great unknowns in the minors. The latest Cuban superprospect might be a great leadoff hitter for the Marlins in the second half, or he might not see the big leagues at all this year. He hasn't played organized ball in a while, and there's sometimes a prolonged adjustment period for Cuban signees. There's undoubtedly a PR reason for the Marlins to call him up, but will he be ready? The odds aren't good.

LUKAS: I'm in the opposite camp, and I fully expect to see Mesa by midseason. The Marlins have made some aggressive promotions, their depth chart is razor thin across the board, and the PR win is just too easy. It's just such a Marlins move to me, rushing a prospect in a year you have no chance just to create some excitement and cover for the fact that your organization has been a consistent letdown (to put it nicely) nearly every year since 2003.

Moreover, it's not as if the Marlins have any other major prospects to leverage during an MLB debut this season. Sixto isn't coming up this year, and barring Harrison suddenly figuring out how not to strike out 40% of the time in Double-A, he isn't either. Diaz will make it up, but he's not even on the top 101 at this point. Alcantara has gotten some run already, negating the novelty factor. And despite the fact that they've traded four really good players over the past two offseasons, that wraps up the entirety of the exciting prospects on the Marlins. Unless you really like pitchability righties.

You already touched on this, but there won't be any exciting trades either. Streckenrider is their best trade piece, but the market doesn't pay a ton for good-not-great relievers at the deadline anymore. If you're the Marlins PR department, you're scratching the bottom of the barrel in terms of creating fan engagement, and unless there are some big internal improvements from Brinson, Alfaro, or others, Mesa is the best option.

NICK: The Marlins PR department probably also wishes that Jeter hadn't removed the dinger machine and brought in better players to field a more palatable team, but that's life I guess. Miami did sign Curtis Granderson, who is one of the most personable guys in baseball, and the team is better off for it. They only gave him a minor league deal, which is an abomination, but yeah. He's another player who will undoubtedly be flipped to a playoff team, and that team will be all the better for having him for his contributions both on and off the field.

If guys like Granderson are only getting minor league deals, why not grab more of them? Why not see what Jim Johnson or Tony Sipp have on the table? Why cut Derek Dietrich when some team can probably use a guy like that on their bench for the stretch run? Again, these aren't players you're going to get the moon for, but it's something. Maybe those guys contribute too much marginal value when you're trying to take advantage of a beefed-up NL East to bank as many losses as possible.

Regardless, the Marlins are going to move some of the guys they have now at the deadline, and they will be a very weird team afterwords. They're going to run Peter O'Brien out in right field to start the year and he might get moved to first base if they tire of his defense and/or they trade Walker. Like you mentioned, Diaz will be up at some point, potentially after a Castro trade clears room for him. Nick Neidert will get chances in the rotation. Flamethrowing Tayron Guerrero might get a shot at the closer's role. Magneuris Sierra will likely get another look in the outfield at some point or another.

Miami Marlins 2019

They'll still be bad. And the wheels on the bus go round and round.

LUKAS: I'd go even more aggressive with the free agency strategy. No reason the Marlins couldn't guarantee Adam Jones $20 million this year and flip him in June, or give Marwin Gonzalez a really front-ended deal. I'm not sure why the whole idea of sign-and-trades hasn't caught on in baseball yet, since it seems like a really good way for rebuilding teams to leverage their financial resources while still giving playing time to young guys who could be a part of the future. Oh, except it costs money, and MLB teams aren't about that.

Seriously though, this team is probably going to be just as bad next year as it is this year. Aside from trading Realmuto for a fine but not incredible return, the Marlins haven't moved their 'rebuild' forward in any way this offseason. We mentioned the guys we like already, but I don't think we or PECOTA expect any of them to be stars or even 3+ WARP guys, and there were only a handful of them to begin with. It's a really bad organization from top to bottom, and that's entirely because the Marlins have decided they're not going to invest a ton of money either on the major league side or into scouting and development.

Moreover, the NL East is just a meat grinder right now. The Mets are in a two year window and 'all-in', the Phillies are actually all in, the Braves are at the start of their window and have an incredible farm, and the Nationals just signed Patrick Corbin and will replace Bryce Harper with Juan Soto and Victor Robles. The Marlins aren't going anywhere for the next five years without significant organizational changes and a commitment to investing in the team.

NICK: The gutting of the scouting department certainly was a bad look, but they've made a few hires in that area over the winter. Still a ways to go, but it's something, I guess? I also would bet on Gary Denbo to do some good building here. They've come up with some interesting finds like Jordan Yamamoto and stocked the upper levels with guys like Zac Gallen who can come up and give you innings if nothing else. Again, they're still not in the forefront of the industry here (which would be helpful when you're starting from scratch!) but I also don't want to act like there's literally no hope for the future.

Given how much the division has improved, I'm actually a little lower on the Marlins than PECOTA. I think guys like Diaz and Neidert, and potentially Mesa, could give the team a nice little boost post-trade deadline. I just don't know that it'll do enough, especially when some of those teams ahead of them will be stocking up too. I'm going to go with 66-98 as their record. That's two losses more than PECOTA sees, which is somewhere near the fudge factor. But this would be boring if I just said "Yeah, that's good."

LUKAS: I really wish I liked them enough to say they'll land at 69, because that's one win above PECOTA. But no, I expect a low 60s win total, mostly because I'm not as bullish on some of the guys as PECOTA is. They'll be picking 2nd in the 2020 draft behind the Orioles, and they'll probably take another prep righty with a straight fastball who promptly blows his arm out. Too bad for them they're only picking fourth this year, since there are three top guys (Bobby Witt, Adley Rutschman, and my dude Andrew Vaughn) and then a drop off. So it goes for the Marlins.

NICK: At least Billy the Marlin is still one of the better mascots in baseball.

Performance Graphs

2018 Hit List Ranking

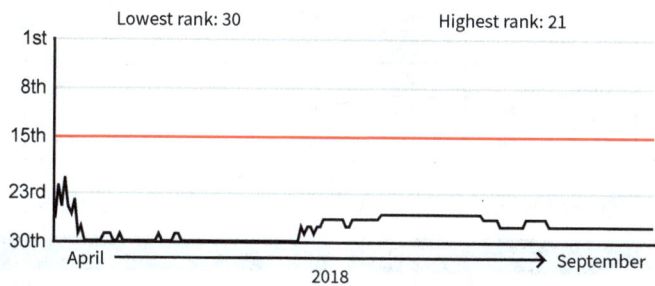

Committed Payroll (in millions)

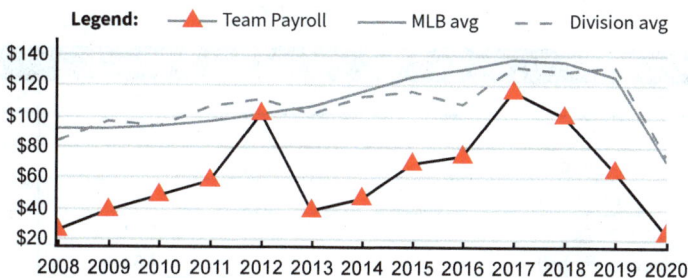

Farm System Ranking

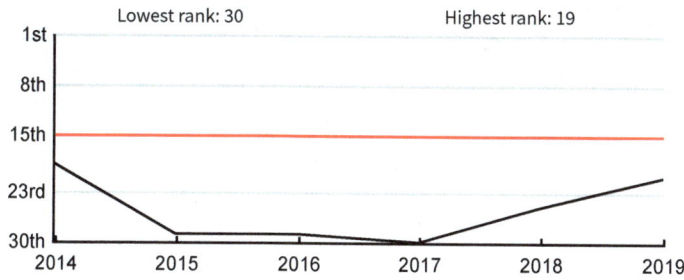

2018 Team Performance

ACTUAL STANDINGS

Team	W	L	Pct
ATL	90	72	.555
WAS	82	80	.506
PHI	80	82	.493
NYN	77	85	.475
MIA	63	98	.391

THIRD-ORDER STANDINGS

Team	W	L	Pct
ATL	94	68	.580
WAS	91	71	.561
NYN	79	83	.487
PHI	79	83	.487
MIA	63	98	.391

TOP HITTERS

Player	WARP
J.T. Realmuto	4.8
JT Riddle	1.8
Brian Anderson	1.8

TOP PITCHERS

Player	WARP
Jose Urena	2.6
Trevor Richards	2.5
Caleb Smith	1.1

VITAL STATISTICS

Statistic Name	Value	Rank
Pythagenpat	.357	29th
Runs Scored per Game	3.66	30th
Runs Allowed per Game	5.02	24th
Deserved Runs Created Plus	86	28th
Deserved Run Average	4.74	22nd
Fielding Independent Pitching	4.52	23rd
Defensive Efficiency Rating	.709	10th
Batter Age	27.5	10th
Pitcher Age	27.3	8th
Salary	$99.5M	23rd
Marginal $ per Marginal Win	$5.9M	7th
Disabled List Days	$1,013.0M	12th
$ on DL	13%	9th

2019 Team Projections

PROJECTED STANDINGS

Team	W	L	Pct	+/-
WAS	89	73	.549	+7
NYN	87	75	.537	+10
ATL	85	77	.524	-5
PHI	85	77	.524	+5
MIA	**68**	**94**	**.419**	**+5**

TOP PROJECTED HITTERS

Player	WARP
Brian Anderson	2.1
Lewis Brinson	1.8
Neil Walker	1.8

TOP PROJECTED PITCHERS

Player	WARP
Nick Neidert	1.1
Jose Urena	1.0
Jordan Yamamoto	0.6

FARM SYSTEM REPORT

Top Prospect	Number of Top 101 Prospects
Sixto Sanchez, #23	3

KEY DEDUCTIONS

Player	WARP
J.T. Realmuto	3.4
Derek Dietrich	1.2
Kyle Barraclough	0.4

KEY ADDITIONS

Player	WARP
Neil Walker	1.8
Curtis Granderson	1.3
Jorge Alfaro	1.1

Team Personnel

President
Michael Hill

Assistant General Manager
Brian Chattin

VP, Player Development & Scouting
Gary Denbo

Director Player Personnel
Daniel Greenlee

Manager
Don Mattingly

BP Alumni
John Eshleman

Marlins Park Stats

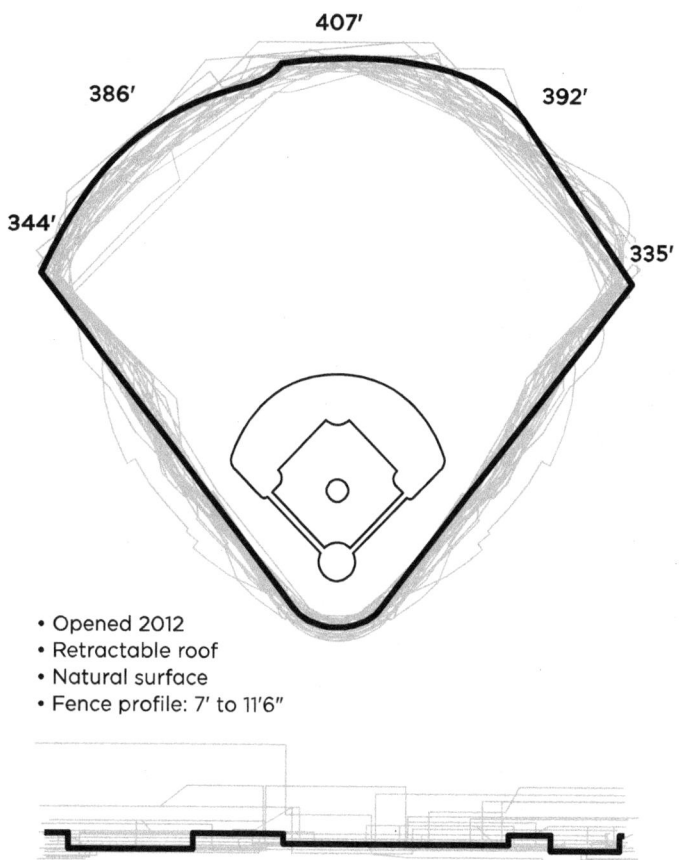

- Opened 2012
- Retractable roof
- Natural surface
- Fence profile: 7' to 11'6"

Three-Year Park Factors

Runs	Runs/RH	Runs/LH	HR/RH	HR/LH
91	91	91	86	93

Marlins Team Analysis

The home run sculpture is gone. "Homer," designed by American artist Red Groom—which means it is capital-A Art—now resides outside the stadium and will be replaced in the park by a three-tier social game-watching area. While fans will get to mill around and sample food and beer, the seven-story home run sculpture will instead hang out on the street like a neon obelisk, marking the end of an era of Miami baseball.

And that's a bummer. The flipping dolphins and flamingos shown in a kaleidoscope of bright colors and flashing lights was such an insane and unique thing to reside in a baseball stadium. It's the kind of installation you'd imagine some megalomaniacal owner would have installed in the 1970s, like when Ewing Kauffman placed a crown over the Royals' center-field. That kind of un-focus-group-tested device seems to be the very opposite of what the Derek Jeter-fronted new Marlins ownership group now represents.

Of course, there could be one other reason why the new owners wanted it gone beyond merely tearing down the most obvious and unmistakable touch of Jeffrey Loria's tenure at the top of the team: The Marlins just didn't hit many home runs. The device exists to revel in the glory of 400-something-foot blasts, and in a post-Stanton world the Marlins hit the fewest in the Majors last year, with only 57 coming at home. Perhaps Jeter looked at the hulking monstrosity as if it were mocking him with its inaction. Maybe when he slept he dreamt of an oceanside pastiche of aquatic animals laughing at him.

But our dear, sweet friend "Homer" wasn't just something beautiful to look at it during a 98-loss Marlins season. It was a seven-story mirror held up to the Marlins' existence.

They are both bright and colorful, piscine, and largely taxpayer-funded. The reason why the art piece wasn't torn down for scrap parts or sent away for prospects was that Miami-Dade County paid $2.5 million for the obelisk. According to MarketWatch, because of bonds and other economics things I'll never understand, the county will have spent about $2.6 billion for Miami's stadium through 2049—which makes "Homer" an absolute steal.

Most importantly, both the team and the sculpture are trapped in an endlessly repeating cycle that can seemingly never be broken. Like Sisyphus pushing his rock up the hill, or Homer Simpson forever returning to Sector 7G no matter what transpired in the preceding half hour, so go the Marlins. Like the fish in "Homer," the Marlins rise, fall, disappear, rise again to win a World Series and then go back

Miami Marlins 2019

under the water to start again. If you believe in reincarnation, then perhaps the team just hasn't learned the lesson that will allow them to move to another stage of existence.

That doesn't just apply to their competitive windows, either. As soon as the postseason ended, the team started promoting their new uniforms with the hashtag #OurColores. While other teams were making moves, the Marlins unveiled a black-blue-and-pinkish rebrand that represented the team's *third* logo and uniform change in their short history. For comparison, the Rockies, who also joined the Majors in 1993, are still rocking the same unis, with a few alternates added to the set. (Oh, and as Craig Mish reported, Billy the Marlin will be getting an update with a smaller bill and thinner body. When you're in South Beach, even your mascot's gotta be fit.)

Unfortunately, while Miami attained the heights of World Series success in 1997 and 2003, they haven't reached the postseason since. Only Seattle has been caught in a longer drought. That's not going to end any time soon for the Marlins, with the team hopefully looking toward 2020—the time that once heralded the age of flying cars and robot maids—for its next competitive window. That's because it wasn't just the home run sculpture that the new owners kicked out of the stadium, but the team's best players, too. The jerseys may change with the whims of each new ownership group, but the prevailing team-building strategy has not.

Here, for those that don't spend every moment thinking of the Marlins rebuilds, is a brief history:

- The 1997 World Series-winning ballclub was dismantled so quickly, the trophy maker probably hadn't laser-etched the names in yet.
- They slashed payroll at the end of the 2005 season and traded Carlos Delgado, Paul Lo Duca, Mike Lowell, Juan Pierre and Josh Beckett in a single go.
- After moving into their new digs in 2011, the team flashed an impressive amount of cash as if to say "We're not the Florida Marlins anymore. We're the *Miami* Marlins." Mark Buehrle, Jose Reyes, and Heath Bell were all signed ... and a year later, none of them were Miami Marlins.

And then last season came with the most WAR traded in a single offseason since the 1899 Louisville Colonels. Marcell Ozuna was sent to the Cardinals, Christian Yelich won the NL MVP and came a game shy of a World Series with the Brewers, and Giancarlo Stanton fulfilled the prophecies when he was shipped to

New York. And now, JT Realmuto-arguably the best catcher in the game—made it clear that he'd be out of Miami the moment free agency allowed it. It's not easy to rebuild when your next generation of stars don't want to be built around.

Those trades weren't the only moves that made it difficult for the local fan base to remember that they're Marlins fans. Despite having one of the most popular players in recent baseball history as the face of the group, one who managed to avoid almost every controversy possible throughout a playing career in a city that feasted on them, Jeter and Co. couldn't help but jump(throw) from scandal to scandal in the early going.

Longtime Marlins and Marlins employees like Jeff Conine were let go. A scout was fired while he was in the hospital receiving cancer treatment. And even Marlins Man, the second-most infamous orange man in America, got in a public fight with Jeter, arguing that he was paying Major League prices for Triple-A talent. He even threatened to wear another team's gear. Shockingly, Jeter didn't bite when he was offered a chance to ride in the "Marlins Car" with Marlins Man to help ingratiate himself to the local fans. Which, honestly, makes me wish there was a two-person sitcom about Jeter and Marlins Man solving petty crimes around Miami in hopes of developing the fanbase. Who wouldn't tune in?

Now that they've cleaned house, it's time to fill the stadium again. To that end, the Marlins seem committed to creating a unique (at least among Major League Baseball teams) fan atmosphere. The new logo is fun in a late-night "Miami Vice" kind of way. Loria may have brought in the Home Run Sculpture and filled the stadium with art (there was even a Roy Lichtenstein hanging on the walls—how many stadiums can claim that?), but now there will be the social area and a standing room only section with cheaper tickets. Looking to create the same atmosphere that has made English soccer and Caribbean Series games so much fun, the space will be replaced with a cheering section complete with fans encouraged to bring flags and musical instruments. It's all in the name of making something that cannot be duplicated from your couch or the bar or while staring at your phone and avoiding conversation at a cocktail party. If successful, this would put the Marlins ahead of the rest of the league, who will likely be trying similar tactics in hopes of getting fans through the turnstiles.

Interestingly enough, it's a kind of reversal from recent marketing efforts that seemed to showcase everything that *wasn't* on the field. Every ballpark features insane Man vs. Food dining options, Kidz Zonez, and enough shops to fill a suburban mall that seem to say, "Hey, there's plenty to do here even if you don't like baseball." Now the Marlins want the biggest fans, the ones who will wave flags and invent chants and songs for the entire lineup, to inspire others to do the same.

The question now is: Where are the fans going to come from?

Miami Marlins 2019

Last year saw attendance drop to just over 10,000 fans a game. That was, in part, because the Marlins changed how they reported ticket sales, but it also was only 700 fans more per night than Loria's old 2004 Expos, who set the record for the lowest per-game attendance in the year before they moved to Washington. This is a new low for a team that has only finished in the top half of NL attendance once—1997—and has finished last for the previous six seasons.

Sure, the team has new ownership and new jerseys and the outfield wall will be painted a new color and fans will get sing to their heart's content, but more than any of that, fans tend to want to watch a winning baseball team. Some fanbases can rally behind a cry of "Trust the Process," but how does one do it when the process is all they've known?

It's not all doom and gloom, and you'll surely see articles soon saying that the Marlins are approaching winning the "right" way—whatever that is. While some may have argued that the teardown didn't need to happen—that a combination of Stanton, Yelich, and Ozuna represented one of the best outfields in the game and was only a few pieces away from contending—the Marlins are now in the league's toughest division. The Braves and Phillies have seen their rebuilds bear fruit and have begun adding the necessary star power to fill the gaps, while the Mets and Nationals are refusing to say goodbye to their own stranglehold atop the division. It's hard to imagine an 85-win team sneaking their way through the division.

So, while the returns for Miami's outfield trio may have been underwhelming, they at least gave the Marlins system plenty of quantity from which a star could emerge. Perhaps it will be Monte Harrison, who hit 19 home runs in Double-A (he also struck out 215 times.) Or maybe Lewis Brinson's abysmal 2017, that saw him hit .199 with a 120/17 K/BB ratio was only the growing pains of a future star. The team also loaded up on international pool money and, in the kind of thing that seems ripped from "Catch-22," landed Cuban star Victor Victor Mesa and his brother Victor Mesa Jr.

Unfortunately, there are no guarantees and prospects are still a crapshoot. For example, the Astros may have found stars in Alex Bregman and Carlos Correa, with Kyle Tucker looking every bit a top-flight prospect, but Jon Singleton, Mark Appel and Francis Martes didn't make the cut despite the once-glowing scouting reports. There are no guarantees that the Marlins' prospects will ever make an impact the way their three-headed home run-hitting monster of an outfield ever did. With more teams trying to create their own super team, the margins are slimmer than ever before, too.

The Marlins are rebuilding. The Marlins have new uniforms and a new direction. You have heard that before and it's happening again. While Marlins fans will hope a third World Series ballclub is coalescing in the minors, the home run sculpture will be watching from outside the stadium. The team is hoping the fans will choose to do it from inside. ■

www.baseballprospectus.com

—*Michael Clair writes for MLB's Cut4.*

Part 2: Player Analysis

Miami Marlins 2019

Jorge Alfaro C
Born: 06/11/93   Age: 26   Bats: R   Throws: R
Height: 6'2"   Weight: 225   Origin: International Free Agent, 2010

YEAR	TEAM	LVL	AGE	PA	R	2B	3B	HR	RBI	BB	K	SB	CS	AVG/OBP/SLG
2016	REA	AA	23	435	68	21	2	15	67	22	105	3	2	.285/.325/.458
2016	PHI	MLB	23	17	0	0	0	0	0	1	8	0	0	.125/.176/.125
2017	LEH	AAA	24	350	34	13	2	7	43	16	113	1	1	.241/.291/.358
2017	PHI	MLB	24	114	12	6	0	5	14	3	33	0	0	.318/.360/.514
2018	PHI	MLB	25	377	35	16	2	10	37	18	138	3	0	.262/.324/.407
2019	MIA	MLB	26	402	40	16	1	9	39	26	123	1	0	.227/.294/.351

Breakout: 9%   Improve: 48%   Collapse: 9%   Attrition: 20%   MLB: 77%
Comparables: Nick Hundley, J.P. Arencibia, Yan Gomes

You're likely to read a lot of "if he could only..." in this chapter. You're bound to come across a few variations on "you can see the potential." It's really only fitting that all of that kicks off with Alfaro, who might be the most tantalizingly talented player on the Phillies roster. No, he hasn't put the whole jigsaw puzzle together yet and, no, he might not put it all together in 2019. It's some comfort knowing that all those pieces are definitely there, even if some are on the other end of the table, a few more are underneath the table, and you just can't seem to find that fourth corner. But improvement was there in 2018 in the form of framing and receiving, along with a more accurate throwing arm, and even some slight decreases in that monstrous K% as the months went by. Alfaro has the raw talent to be an absolute force on both sides of the ball, but it's fair to wonder if he'll realize it before it's too late.

YEAR	TEAM	P. COUNT	FRM RUNS	BLK RUNS	THRW RUNS	TOT RUNS
2016	PHI	576	0.0	-0.6	0.0	-0.4
2017	LEH	10516	2.0	-0.5	0.3	0.9
2017	PHI	4051	-2.6	0.2	-0.1	-2.9
2018	PHI	14100	12.3	-2.4	0.0	10.2
2019	MIA	15139	5.5	-1.5	0.3	4.3

YEAR	TEAM	LVL	AGE	PA	DRC+	VORP	BABIP	BRR	FRAA	WARP
2016	REA	AA	23	435	109	20.9	.347	-1.5	C(95): 14.8	3.2
2016	PHI	MLB	23	17	57	-2.5	.250	-0.1	C(4): -0.6	-0.1
2017	LEH	AAA	24	350	73	4.4	.345	-1.4	C(77): 4.8	0.4
2017	PHI	MLB	24	114	93	10.7	.420	-1.5	C(28): -2.5, 1B(2): 0.1	0.1
2018	PHI	MLB	25	377	84	24.2	.406	0.5	C(104): 12.2, 3B(1): 0.0	2.5
2019	MIA	MLB	26	402	80	8.7	.316	-0.5	C4	1.1

Jorge Alfaro, continued

Batted Ball Distribution

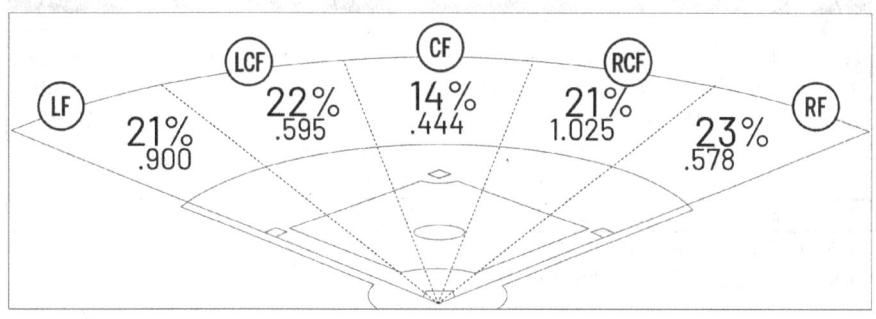

LF	LCF	CF	RCF	RF
21% .900	22% .595	14% .444	21% 1.025	23% .578

Strike Zone vs LHP   **Strike Zone vs RHP**

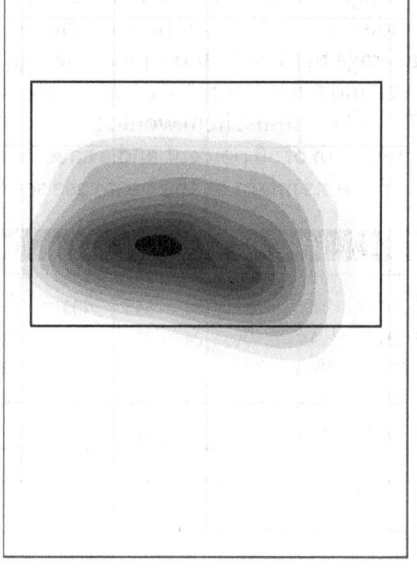

Miami Marlins 2019

Brian Anderson 3B

Born: 05/19/93   Age: 26   Bats: R   Throws: R
Height: 6'3"   Weight: 185   Origin: Round 3, 2014 Draft (#76 overall)

YEAR	TEAM	LVL	AGE	PA	R	2B	3B	HR	RBI	BB	K	SB	CS	AVG/OBP/SLG
2016	JUP	A+	23	207	27	12	2	3	25	22	38	3	0	.302/.377/.440
2016	JAX	AA	23	345	38	9	1	8	40	36	59	0	0	.243/.330/.359
2017	JAX	AA	24	361	53	14	3	14	55	36	71	1	1	.251/.341/.450
2017	NWO	AAA	24	137	21	7	0	8	26	12	27	0	1	.339/.416/.602
2017	MIA	MLB	24	95	11	7	1	0	8	10	28	0	0	.262/.337/.369
2018	MIA	MLB	25	670	87	34	4	11	65	62	129	2	4	.273/.357/.400
2019	MIA	MLB	26	600	72	28	3	13	58	56	122	2	2	.259/.342/.398

Breakout: 13%   Improve: 41%   Collapse: 6%   Attrition: 13%   MLB: 84%
Comparables: Stephen Piscotty, Chris Parmelee, Shin-Soo Choo

There weren't many big-league bright spots for the Marlins last season, but Anderson was certainly one of them. He proved to be durable, starting all but six games on the season, and his bat, though lacking in thump, played consistently enough that he wasn't a detriment in the lineup. On a forgettable team, Anderson's rookie campaign became an afterthought, but his ability to play an average third base and a passable right field, walk at a slightly above-average rate and temper his strikeouts creates the foundation for a consistent regular. The one wish-list item would be to hit for more power, but with a ground-ball rate north of 50 percent and a cavernous ballpark to call home, a season with 15 home runs might be the best-case scenario.

YEAR	TEAM	LVL	AGE	PA	DRC+	VORP	BABIP	BRR	FRAA	WARP
2016	JUP	A+	23	207	154	13.9	.364	-1.5	3B(47): 8.5	2.1
2016	JAX	AA	23	345	103	13.7	.274	0.2	3B(85): 12.7	2.0
2017	JAX	AA	24	361	113	19.8	.277	-1.3	3B(82): 9.0	1.8
2017	NWO	AAA	24	137	167	20.8	.376	-0.4	3B(30): 1.5	1.5
2017	MIA	MLB	24	95	66	4.6	.386	1.0	3B(25): -2.2	-0.2
2018	MIA	MLB	25	670	109	43.2	.332	2.3	RF(91): -1.1, 3B(71): -9.0	1.8
2019	MIA	MLB	26	600	108	24.4	.311	-1.2	3B 2, RF -1	2.1

Brian Anderson, continued

Batted Ball Distribution

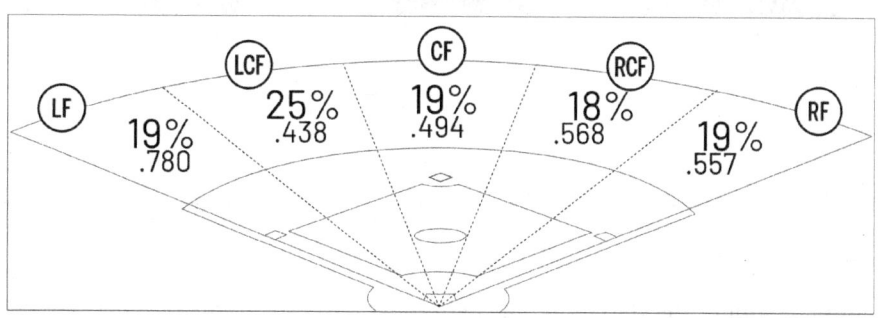

Strike Zone vs LHP   **Strike Zone vs RHP**

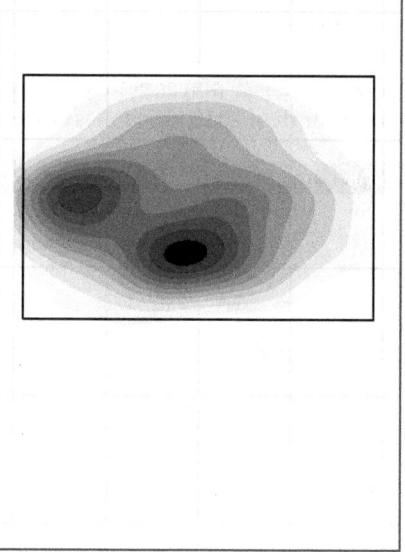

Lewis Brinson CF

Born: 05/08/94 Age: 25 Bats: R Throws: R
Height: 6'3" Weight: 195 Origin: Round 1, 2012 Draft (#29 overall)

YEAR	TEAM	LVL	AGE	PA	R	2B	3B	HR	RBI	BB	K	SB	CS	AVG/OBP/SLG
2016	FRI	AA	22	326	46	14	6	11	40	17	64	11	4	.237/.280/.431
2016	CSP	AAA	22	93	14	9	0	4	20	2	21	4	2	.382/.387/.618
2017	MIL	MLB	23	55	2	0	1	2	3	7	17	1	0	.106/.236/.277
2017	CSP	AAA	23	340	66	22	4	13	48	32	62	11	5	.331/.400/.562
2018	MIA	MLB	24	406	31	10	5	11	42	17	120	2	1	.199/.240/.338
2019	MIA	MLB	25	475	53	22	3	13	51	27	124	7	3	.244/.293/.396

Breakout: 15% Improve: 50% Collapse: 12% Attrition: 34% MLB: 85%
Comparables: Brian Anderson, Ryan Kalish, Kirk Nieuwenhuis

By all accounts, the Marlins did the right thing with Lewis Brinson — they let him play. But an OPS that couldn't cross the .600 mark stings more when you were the headliner of the trade that sent away the MVP. However, Brinson needed the major-league reps after showing he was done mastering Triple-A. The Florida native struggled mightily in every facet of the game, including defense, the part that was supposed to make up for his rawness at the plate. The impact profile is still there. His plus speed and power haven't disappeared and the ceiling remains a 25-25 player at peak. But even with a marginal improvement in the final month of 2018, Brinson is still very much a work in progress.

YEAR	TEAM	LVL	AGE	PA	DRC+	VORP	BABIP	BRR	FRAA	WARP
2016	FRI	AA	22	326	76	3.6	.264	-0.4	CF(65): -0.2, RF(5): -1.1	-0.8
2016	CSP	AAA	22	93	140	8.9	.455	-0.1	CF(23): 6.0	1.2
2017	MIL	MLB	23	55	73	-3.4	.107	-0.5	LF(8): -0.1, CF(8): 0.4	0.0
2017	CSP	AAA	23	340	131	27.2	.377	1.6	CF(61): 1.1, LF(6): 3.2	2.5
2018	MIA	MLB	24	406	64	-5.2	.257	-0.9	CF(106): 3.3	-0.1
2019	MIA	MLB	25	475	92	13.5	.308	0.2	CF 5	1.8

Lewis Brinson, continued

Batted Ball Distribution

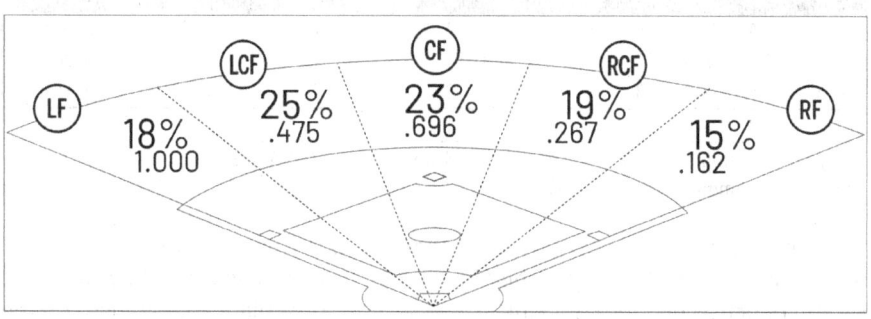

Strike Zone vs LHP   **Strike Zone vs RHP**

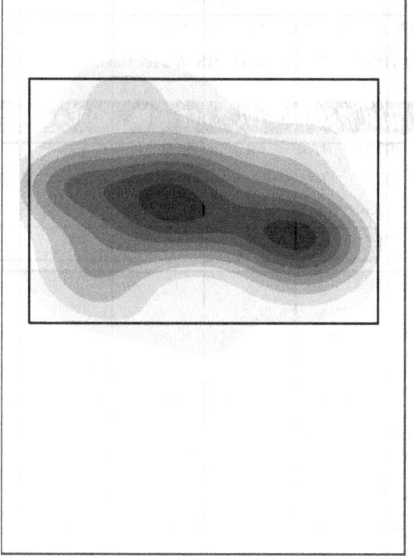

Miami Marlins 2019

Starlin Castro 2B

Born: 03/24/90   Age: 29   Bats: R   Throws: R
Height: 6'2"   Weight: 230   Origin: International Free Agent, 2006

YEAR	TEAM	LVL	AGE	PA	R	2B	3B	HR	RBI	BB	K	SB	CS	AVG/OBP/SLG
2016	NYA	MLB	26	610	63	29	1	21	70	24	118	4	0	.270/.300/.433
2017	NYA	MLB	27	473	66	18	1	16	63	23	93	2	0	.300/.338/.454
2018	MIA	MLB	28	647	76	32	2	12	54	48	124	6	4	.278/.329/.400
2019	MIA	MLB	29	561	58	25	2	12	60	40	108	4	2	.263/.320/.390

Breakout: 2%   Improve: 47%   Collapse: 15%   Attrition: 4%   MLB: 100%
Comparables: Jimmie Reese, Omar Infante, Howie Kendrick

You likely forgot that Castro played for the Marlins last year. There were times where Castro himself surely wished he'd forget he was playing for the Marlins. He still punched his clock, racking up the second-most plate appearances on the team, splitting his time among the first three spots in the order. As expected, most of his counting stats suffered thanks to a barren lineup and a huge ballpark. Castro did marginally improve in one part of his game that caused a ripple effect, swinging less often overall and refusing to chase pitches while maintaining the same contact rate. He saw curveballs better than before, and as a result he ticked his walk rate to a career-best 7.4 percent.

YEAR	TEAM	LVL	AGE	PA	DRC+	VORP	BABIP	BRR	FRAA	WARP
2016	NYA	MLB	26	610	93	8.1	.305	-2.1	2B(150): 1.3, SS(3): -0.5	1.1
2017	NYA	MLB	27	473	102	18.2	.347	0.5	2B(109): -4.9	1.1
2018	MIA	MLB	28	647	102	31.4	.330	0.3	2B(150): -6.2	1.6
2019	MIA	MLB	29	561	97	17.8	.310	-0.8	2B -4	1.3

Starlin Castro, continued

Batted Ball Distribution

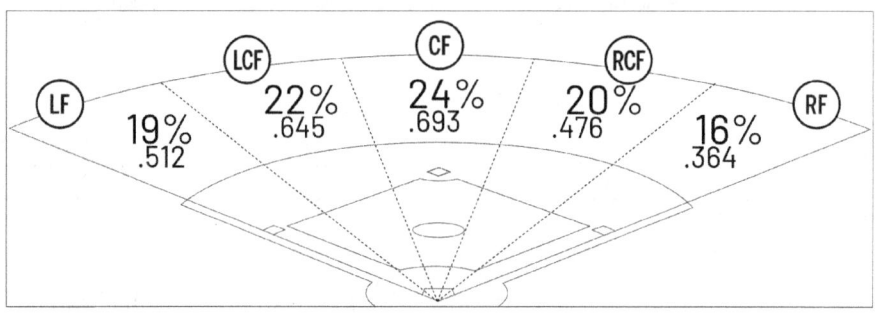

Strike Zone vs LHP

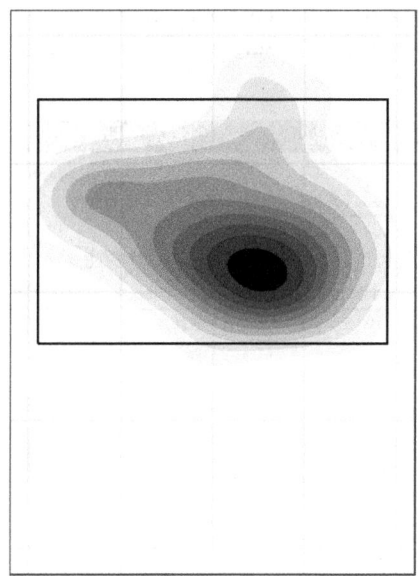

Strike Zone vs RHP

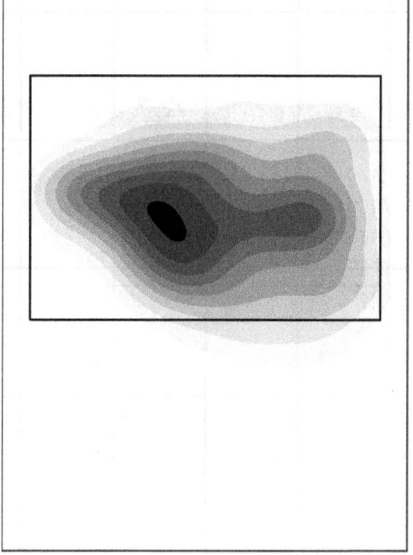

Austin Dean LF

Born: 10/14/93 Age: 25 Bats: R Throws: R
Height: 6'1" Weight: 190 Origin: Round 4, 2012 Draft (#137 overall)

YEAR	TEAM	LVL	AGE	PA	R	2B	3B	HR	RBI	BB	K	SB	CS	AVG/OBP/SLG
2016	JAX	AA	22	536	60	23	5	11	67	48	110	1	2	.238/.307/.375
2017	JAX	AA	23	251	29	14	4	4	30	14	46	3	1	.282/.323/.427
2018	JAX	AA	24	88	13	8	1	3	14	6	7	0	0	.420/.466/.654
2018	NWO	AAA	24	358	58	12	4	9	54	33	49	2	2	.326/.397/.475
2018	MIA	MLB	24	122	16	4	0	4	14	7	22	1	0	.221/.279/.363
2019	MIA	MLB	25	403	43	14	3	10	46	30	72	1	0	.268/.332/.405

Breakout: 7% Improve: 38% Collapse: 6% Attrition: 32% MLB: 68%
Comparables: Austin Slater, Zoilo Almonte, Caleb Gindl

Considering they assigned him to Double-A for a third straight year, the Marlins were likely unenthusiastic about Dean entering 2018. But after his absurd start in Double-A and an exceptional stint in Triple-A, the team finally felt he was worth the gamble and called him up. Dean, who exists in the unfortunate void where he isn't fast enough to be a center fielder and may not possesses enough game power to cut it as an everyday corner guy, will likely recede into the Land of Fourth Outfielder.

YEAR	TEAM	LVL	AGE	PA	DRC+	VORP	BABIP	BRR	FRAA	WARP
2016	JAX	AA	22	536	94	8.6	.283	-0.5	LF(115): 3.3, RF(1): -0.1	0.1
2017	JAX	AA	23	251	105	14.4	.333	0.9	LF(53): -2.8, RF(3): -0.5	-0.1
2018	JAX	AA	24	88	197	12.5	.437	-2.0	LF(21): 0.5	0.8
2018	NWO	AAA	24	358	135	31.0	.360	0.5	LF(45): -2.2, RF(37): -0.8	1.5
2018	MIA	MLB	24	122	93	1.5	.241	1.1	LF(31): 0.5	0.4
2019	MIA	MLB	25	403	107	15.8	.304	-0.3	LF 0	1.6

Austin Dean, continued

Batted Ball Distribution

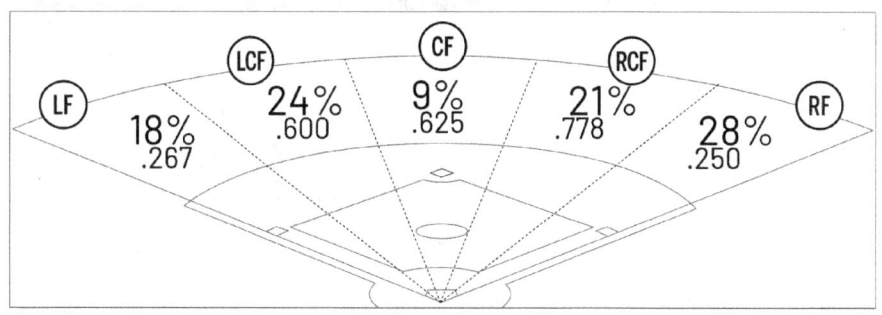

| | Strike Zone vs LHP | Strike Zone vs RHP |

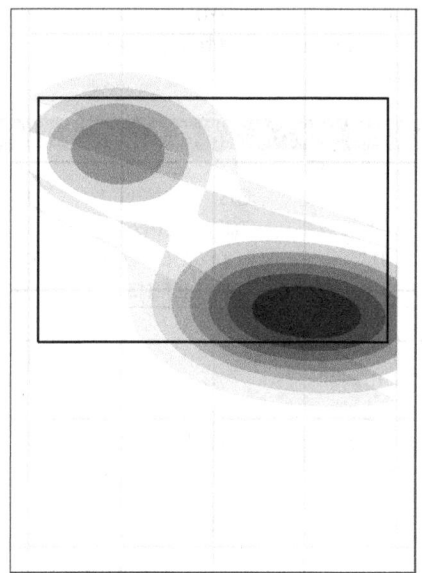
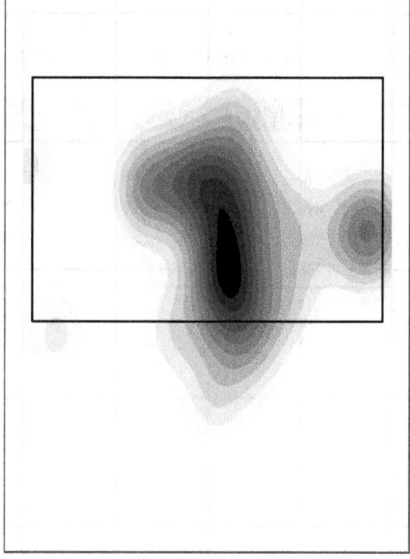

Miami Marlins 2019

Isaac Galloway   OF

Born: 10/10/89   Age: 29   Bats: R   Throws: R
Height: 6'2"   Weight: 205   Origin: Round 8, 2008 Draft (#238 overall)

YEAR	TEAM	LVL	AGE	PA	R	2B	3B	HR	RBI	BB	K	SB	CS	AVG/OBP/SLG
2016	NWO	AAA	26	486	61	19	2	10	38	33	112	31	10	.254/.312/.374
2017	JAX	AA	27	49	4	5	0	0	3	6	8	5	2	.405/.490/.524
2017	NWO	AAA	27	83	12	0	0	7	16	7	21	5	0	.280/.349/.560
2018	NWO	AAA	28	356	64	21	3	9	30	21	75	20	7	.262/.315/.429
2018	MIA	MLB	28	74	7	3	0	3	7	9	21	1	1	.203/.301/.391
2019	MIA	MLB	29	35	4	1	0	1	3	2	9	1	0	.219/.265/.344

Breakout: 1%   Improve: 6%   Collapse: 12%   Attrition: 21%   MLB: 27%
Comparables: Jim Adduci, Moises Sierra, Reid Gorecki

Isaac Galloway's name resembles that of a forlorn philosopher cast aside for his poppycock theories of Living Organisms on the Sun. Alas, the Galloway we know has also been cast aside in baseball, making a hard living in the minor leagues for the last 10 years. In fact, it wasn't until July 31 of last year that he made his major-league debut at the ripe age of 28. He even hit a walk-off double in late September. But it's memories like that Galloway must cling to because ultimately he's just there for organizational depth.

YEAR	TEAM	LVL	AGE	PA	DRC+	VORP	BABIP	BRR	FRAA	WARP
2016	NWO	AAA	26	486	85	19.1	.318	3.3	CF(57): -1.9, RF(48): 5.5	0.6
2017	JAX	AA	27	49	172	6.8	.500	0.5	CF(5): -0.8, LF(2): 0.3	0.4
2017	NWO	AAA	27	83	127	8.5	.298	0.4	CF(19): -0.6, LF(2): 0.0	0.4
2018	NWO	AAA	28	356	92	22.9	.314	9.5	RF(59): -0.2, CF(22): -1.6	0.9
2018	MIA	MLB	28	74	86	1.7	.250	0.4	LF(18): -0.8, RF(13): 1.3	0.2
2019	MIA	MLB	29	35	58	-0.6	.280	0.1	LF 1	0.0

Isaac Galloway, continued

Batted Ball Distribution

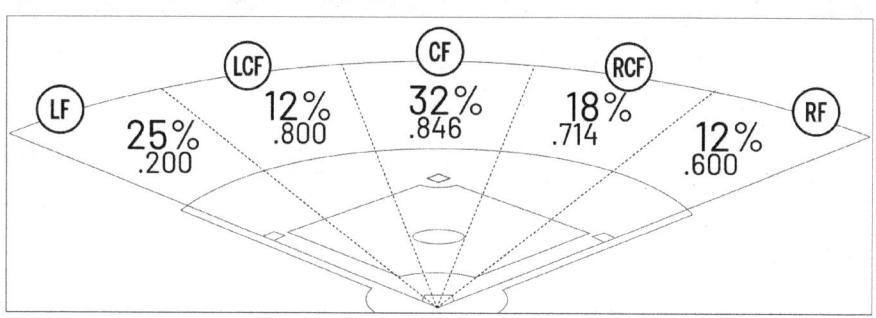

| Strike Zone vs LHP | Strike Zone vs RHP |

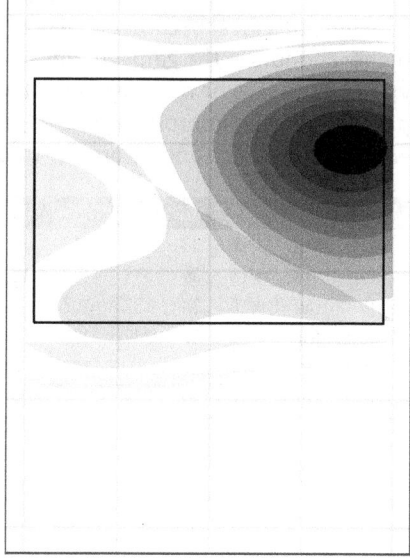

Miami Marlins 2019

Curtis Granderson RF
Born: 03/16/81 Age: 38 Bats: L Throws: R
Height: 6'1" Weight: 200 Origin: Round 3, 2002 Draft (#80 overall)

YEAR	TEAM	LVL	AGE	PA	R	2B	3B	HR	RBI	BB	K	SB	CS	AVG/OBP/SLG
2016	NYN	MLB	35	633	88	24	5	30	59	74	130	4	2	.237/.335/.464
2017	NYN	MLB	36	395	58	22	3	19	52	53	90	4	2	.228/.334/.481
2017	LAN	MLB	36	132	16	2	0	7	12	18	33	2	0	.161/.288/.366
2018	TOR	MLB	37	349	48	21	1	11	35	42	96	2	1	.245/.342/.430
2018	MIL	MLB	37	54	12	1	1	2	3	12	10	0	0	.220/.407/.439
2019	MIA	MLB	38	543	70	24	2	18	58	57	126	5	2	.229/.315/.401

Breakout: 0% Improve: 11% Collapse: 31% Attrition: 22% MLB: 73%
Comparables: Ken Griffey, Joe Harris, Larry Walker

The "Curtis Granderson Scale" could update the "Kenny Lofton Scale": this scale weighs the point at which an elite player becomes less known for their overall career success and more for their desirable characteristics to help win a title through midseason acquisitions. Granderson has more than 40 career WARP, and Lofton was near a similar total when he began his playoff mercenary phase. Reaching this level of career achievement should be viewed as one of the highest honors in the game; teams want YOU! to contend. Granderson did not waste his shot to be a winner with Milwaukee, providing crucial walks and power during an improbable late-season stretch. Those desirable veteran traits wait in the balance once more, for trade or hire during the next playoff run.

YEAR	TEAM	LVL	AGE	PA	DRC+	VORP	BABIP	BRR	FRAA	WARP
2016	NYN	MLB	35	633	112	37.7	.254	1.3	RF(110): 3.1, CF(36): -4.4	2.5
2017	NYN	MLB	36	395	107	26.5	.251	1.5	CF(59): -8.4, RF(30): 1.9	1.0
2017	LAN	MLB	36	132	107	3.0	.153	0.2	LF(26): -3.2, RF(8): 0.2	0.2
2018	TOR	MLB	37	349	100	8.2	.321	-2.3	LF(41): 0.5, RF(31): -1.9	0.4
2018	MIL	MLB	37	54	100	3.3	.241	-0.5	RF(14): -0.5, LF(3): -0.1	0.0
2019	MIA	MLB	38	543	99	16.1	.273	-0.5	RF 1, LF -1	1.3

Curtis Granderson, continued

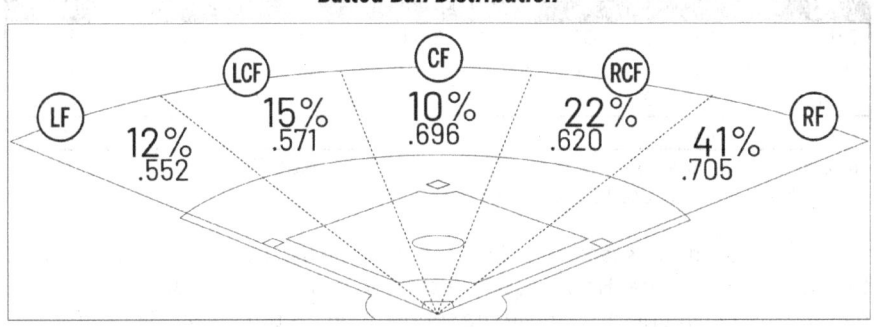

Batted Ball Distribution

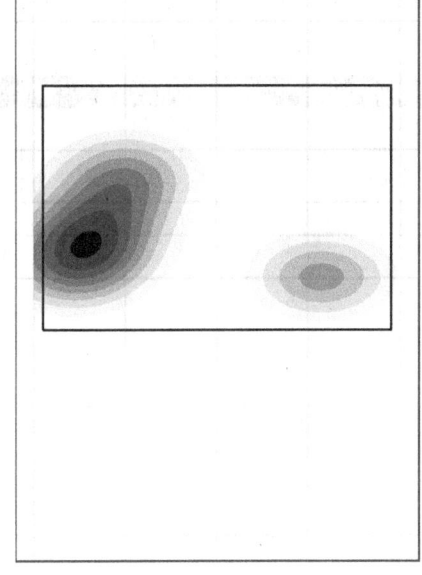

Strike Zone vs LHP

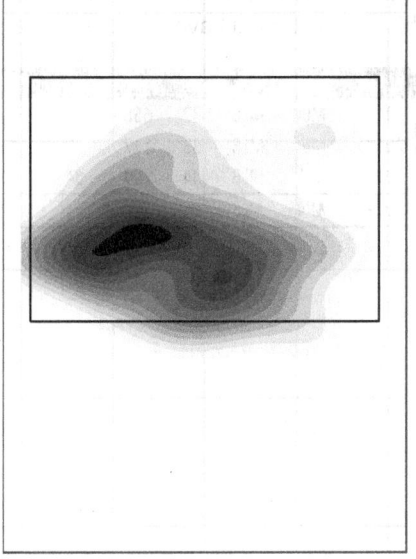

Strike Zone vs RHP

Martin Prado 3B

Born: 10/27/83 Age: 35 Bats: R Throws: R
Height: 6'0" Weight: 215 Origin: International Free Agent, 2001

YEAR	TEAM	LVL	AGE	PA	R	2B	3B	HR	RBI	BB	K	SB	CS	AVG/OBP/SLG
2016	MIA	MLB	32	658	70	37	3	8	75	49	69	2	2	.305/.359/.417
2017	MIA	MLB	33	147	13	9	0	2	12	6	22	0	0	.250/.279/.357
2018	MIA	MLB	34	209	16	9	0	1	18	11	35	1	1	.244/.287/.305
2019	MIA	MLB	35	277	30	14	1	4	24	20	44	1	1	.265/.321/.375

Breakout: 1%   Improve: 15%   Collapse: 17%   Attrition: 23%   MLB: 78%
Comparables: Aaron Hill, Yunel Escobar, Placido Polanco

It's been a horrid two seasons for Prado, one of the most beloved presences in the Marlins' clubhouse. He's amassed just 91 games since the start of 2017, battling myriad injuries that make the spotlight on his three-year, $40 million contract grow harsher and harsher. Last season, after recovering from right knee surgery in the offseason, he strained his left hamstring, his left quad, and for good measure, his right abdominal. With a deteriorating glove and a punchless bat, Prado has very little left to give. But with $15 million left on the final year of his contract, he'll have to provide value somewhere.

YEAR	TEAM	LVL	AGE	PA	DRC+	VORP	BABIP	BRR	FRAA	WARP
2016	MIA	MLB	32	658	111	39.9	.331	0.2	3B(150): -3.1	2.9
2017	MIA	MLB	33	147	79	-2.2	.282	-1.0	3B(34): -1.2	-0.1
2018	MIA	MLB	34	209	84	1.2	.292	0.4	3B(48): -4.5, 1B(1): 0.1	-0.1
2019	MIA	MLB	35	277	94	5.8	.301	-0.5	3B -1, LF 0	0.3

Martin Prado, continued

Batted Ball Distribution

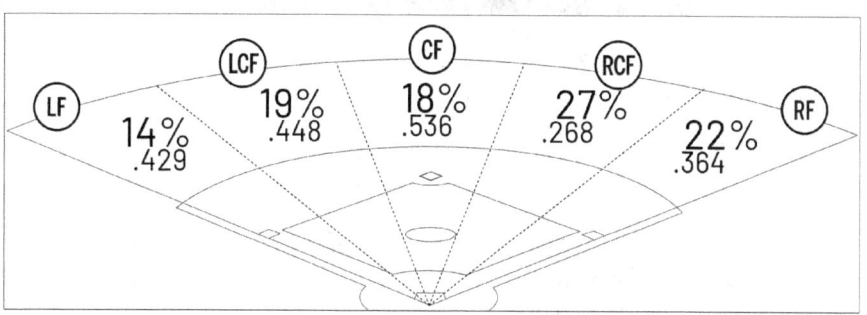

Strike Zone vs LHP   Strike Zone vs RHP

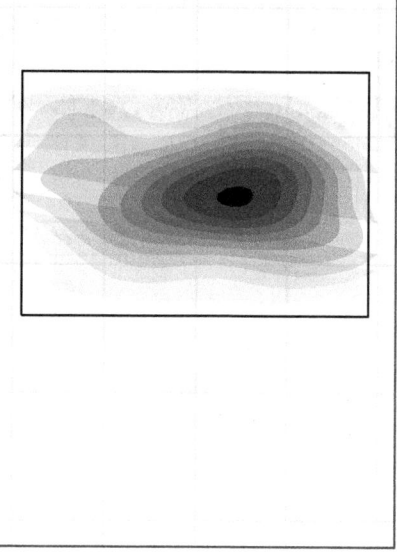

Miguel Rojas INF

Born: 02/24/89 Age: 30 Bats: R Throws: R
Height: 5'11" Weight: 195 Origin: International Free Agent, 2005

YEAR	TEAM	LVL	AGE	PA	R	2B	3B	HR	RBI	BB	K	SB	CS	AVG/OBP/SLG
2016	MIA	MLB	27	214	27	12	0	1	14	11	27	2	1	.247/.288/.325
2017	MIA	MLB	28	306	37	16	2	1	26	27	32	2	1	.290/.361/.375
2018	MIA	MLB	29	527	44	13	0	11	53	24	69	6	3	.252/.297/.346
2019	MIA	MLB	30	320	33	13	1	5	29	24	45	3	2	.254/.319/.359

Breakout: 1% Improve: 35% Collapse: 9% Attrition: 18% MLB: 89%
Comparables: Ryan Theriot, Brendan Ryan, Paul Janish

One of the Marlins' fetishes is strong defensive infielders who are an active detriment when at the plate. For the last four years Rojas has been one of several phone calls the Fish make to satiate their needs, and last season his profile was on full display. Though most of his time came at shortstop and third base, he also saw time at first base and second base, showcasing an exceptional glove at each position. The light-hitting utility man has a knack for making contact and limiting strikeouts, but it doesn't help his production. But for the Marlins, his skills are always going to be just enough to make them bite their lower lip.

YEAR	TEAM	LVL	AGE	PA	DRC+	VORP	BABIP	BRR	FRAA	WARP
2016	MIA	MLB	27	214	75	-2.1	.280	0.7	2B(45): -0.6, 1B(41): 1.8	0.6
2017	MIA	MLB	28	306	92	21.0	.324	4.6	SS(77): -0.2, 3B(15): -0.2	1.5
2018	MIA	MLB	29	527	90	8.8	.272	-2.5	SS(83): 5.4, 1B(49): -0.3	1.6
2019	MIA	MLB	30	320	86	6.2	.281	-0.5	SS 2, 1B 1	0.7

Miguel Rojas, continued

Batted Ball Distribution

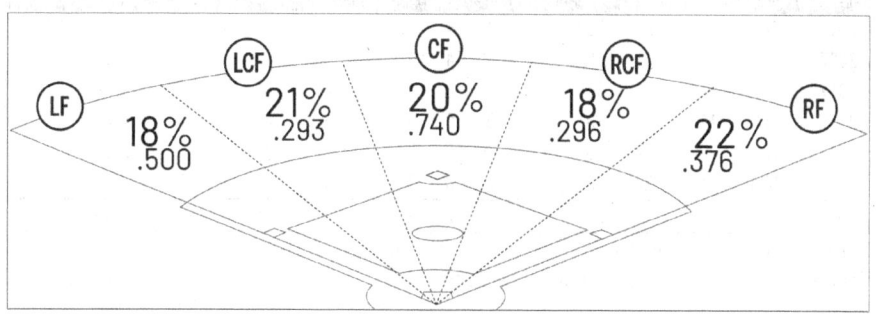

Strike Zone vs LHP

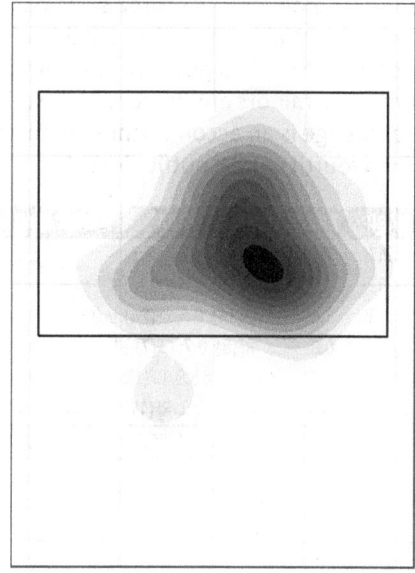

Strike Zone vs RHP

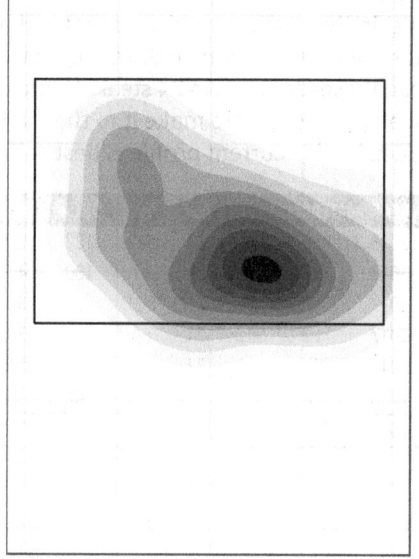

Miami Marlins 2019

Magneuris Sierra CF
Born: 04/07/96 Age: 23 Bats: L Throws: L
Height: 5'11" Weight: 160 Origin: International Free Agent, 2012

YEAR	TEAM	LVL	AGE	PA	R	2B	3B	HR	RBI	BB	K	SB	CS	AVG/OBP/SLG
2016	PEO	A	20	562	78	29	4	3	60	22	97	31	17	.307/.335/.395
2017	PMB	A+	21	89	16	3	4	0	9	7	15	3	5	.272/.337/.407
2017	SFD	AA	21	353	32	18	3	1	35	20	59	17	5	.269/.313/.352
2017	SLN	MLB	21	64	10	0	0	0	5	4	14	2	2	.317/.359/.317
2018	NWO	AAA	22	367	48	12	5	2	17	13	73	14	5	.260/.287/.341
2018	MIA	MLB	22	156	10	3	0	0	7	6	39	3	2	.190/.222/.211
2019	MIA	MLB	23	243	23	8	2	4	22	11	55	6	3	.225/.264/.330

Breakout: 18% Improve: 26% Collapse: 1% Attrition: 12% MLB: 28%
Comparables: Eury Perez, Charlie Tilson, Engel Beltre

Last year was a significant step back for Sierra, one of the centerpieces in the Marcell Ozuna trade. Lauded for his speed and defense, he had a rough time showcasing either, especially during a major-league stint in which he hobbled to a .433 OPS, worst in baseball. The slapstick hitter managed just three extra-base hits in that span and showed that he had no self-restraint on pitches outside of the zone. Even when he did get on base, his instincts lacked polish, as he got caught seven times in 24 steal attempts across the minors and majors. He's still really young, and to make it to the majors at his age is an accomplishment on its own, but his current profile is best suited for a fourth or fifth outfielder role.

YEAR	TEAM	LVL	AGE	PA	DRC+	VORP	BABIP	BRR	FRAA	WARP
2016	PEO	A	20	562	122	28.9	.367	1.6	CF(121): 3.3	2.8
2017	PMB	A+	21	89	100	4.2	.333	1.1	CF(19): 0.6	0.3
2017	SFD	AA	21	353	83	3.6	.323	3.6	RF(34): 0.5, LF(26): 2.0	0.2
2017	SLN	MLB	21	64	78	3.1	.413	0.8	RF(8): 0.7, CF(7): -1.3	0.0
2018	NWO	AAA	22	367	61	5.8	.322	3.2	CF(81): 5.8, RF(1): 0.7	0.2
2018	MIA	MLB	22	156	40	-1.2	.259	-0.4	CF(32): -0.3, RF(19): -0.1	-0.8
2019	MIA	MLB	23	243	64	-1.6	.275	0.4	CF -1, RF 2	-0.2

Magneuris Sierra, continued

Batted Ball Distribution

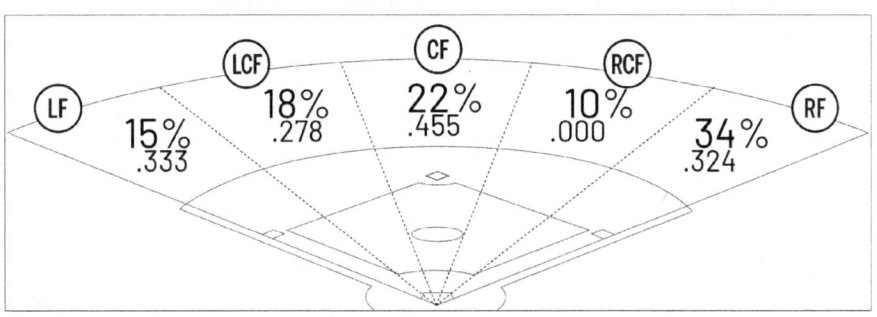

Strike Zone vs LHP   Strike Zone vs RHP

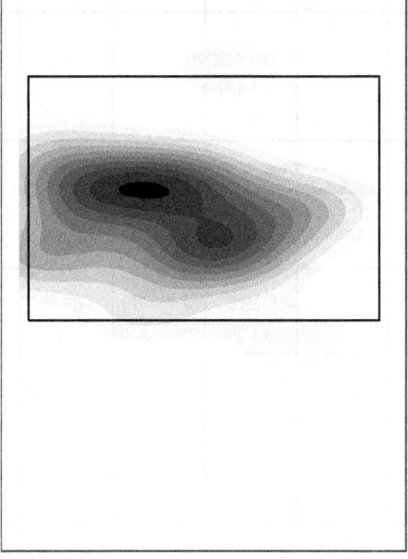

Miami Marlins 2019

Neil Walker 2B

Born: 09/10/85 Age: 33 Bats: B Throws: R
Height: 6'3" Weight: 210 Origin: Round 1, 2004 Draft (#11 overall)

YEAR	TEAM	LVL	AGE	PA	R	2B	3B	HR	RBI	BB	K	SB	CS	AVG/OBP/SLG
2016	NYN	MLB	30	458	57	9	1	23	55	42	84	3	1	.282/.347/.476
2017	NYN	MLB	31	299	40	13	2	10	36	27	47	0	1	.264/.339/.442
2017	MIL	MLB	31	149	19	8	0	4	13	28	30	0	1	.267/.409/.433
2018	NYA	MLB	32	398	48	12	1	11	46	42	87	0	0	.219/.309/.354
2019	MIA	MLB	33	470	52	20	2	12	50	45	92	1	1	.252/.330/.397

Breakout: 0% Improve: 28% Collapse: 15% Attrition: 13% MLB: 92%
Comparables: Aubrey Huff, Lyle Overbay, Tino Martinez

The Yankees always have one move a year that could be classified as "good process, bad result." Last year was Matt Holliday, who was fairly competent until contracting Epstein-Barr, and this year the title goes to Neil Walker. The veteran was brought in late in spring training as insurance for resident neophytes Gleyber Torres and Miguel Andujar, and his $4 million deal fit the bill. Walker subsequently posted career lows in home runs, isolated power, hits, and a career high in his strikeout rate. Wherever he finds himself, Walker will be a prime rebound candidate to at least split the difference between his worst year and his baseline from 2014-16. He'll also likely be waiting for the call most of another winter.

YEAR	TEAM	LVL	AGE	PA	DRC+	VORP	BABIP	BRR	FRAA	WARP
2016	NYN	MLB	30	458	124	31.2	.302	0.3	2B(111): 2.6	3.0
2017	NYN	MLB	31	299	107	12.6	.286	-1.5	2B(68): -5.0, 1B(3): 0.0	0.5
2017	MIL	MLB	31	149	108	10.0	.326	-0.7	2B(27): -1.1, 1B(14): 0.0	0.4
2018	NYA	MLB	32	398	89	-0.5	.257	-1.0	1B(42): 4.2, 2B(32): 0.7	0.7
2019	MIA	MLB	33	470	103	12.8	.295	-0.8	1B 6, 3B 0	1.8

Neil Walker, continued

Batted Ball Distribution

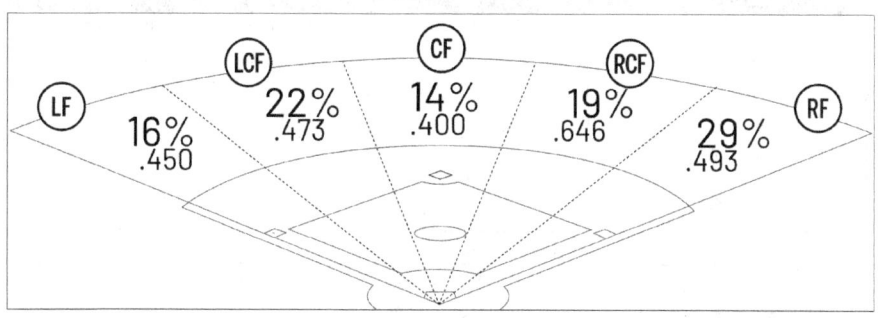

Strike Zone vs LHP

Strike Zone vs RHP

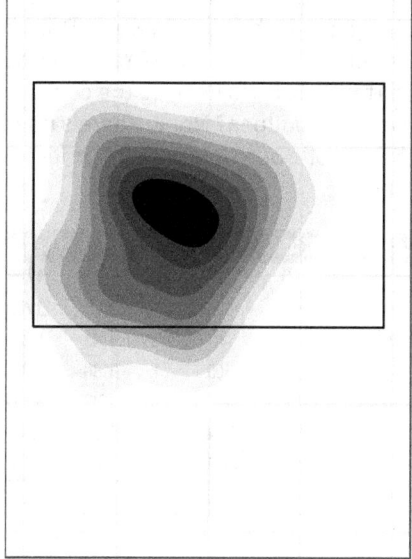

Miami Marlins 2019

Sandy Alcantara   RHP

Born: 09/07/95   Age: 23   Bats: R   Throws: R
Height: 6'4"   Weight: 170   Origin: International Free Agent, 2013

YEAR	TEAM	LVL	AGE	W	L	SV	G	GS	IP	H	HR	BB/9	K/9	K	GB%	BABIP
2016	PEO	A	20	5	7	0	17	17	90^1	78	4	4.5	11.9	119	46%	.333
2016	PMB	A+	20	0	4	0	6	6	32^1	25	0	3.9	9.5	34	52%	.294
2017	SFD	AA	21	7	5	0	25	22	125^1	125	13	3.9	7.6	106	46%	.305
2017	SLN	MLB	21	0	0	0	8	0	8^1	9	2	6.5	10.8	10	26%	.333
2018	JUP	A+	22	0	0	0	3	3	11^1	10	0	4.0	6.4	8	62%	.294
2018	NWO	AAA	22	6	3	0	19	19	115^2	107	10	3.0	6.8	88	50%	.283
2018	MIA	MLB	22	2	3	0	6	6	34	25	3	6.1	7.9	30	50%	.250
2019	MIA	MLB	23	3	5	0	13	13	68	63	8	3.9	8.3	63	45%	.289

Breakout: 17%   Improve: 26%   Collapse: 15%   Attrition: 36%   MLB: 57%
Comparables: Jake Thompson, Archie Bradley, Scott Barnes

The same questions that dogged Alcantara a couple of years ago are still dogging him today. His big, upper-90s fastball is still a plus-plus pitch that has sink and run, and he deploys the four-seam and two-seam variety. His slider and changeup flash above average. Does he have the frame to grow into and become an innings eater? Yes. Does he have the raw stuff to become a no. 3 starter? Yes. Does he have the command and control to definitively say he can avoid the bullpen? Nope. There's no reason to sound an alarm on him yet, but the realistic outcome is perhaps less rosy than when the Marlins first acquired him.

YEAR	TEAM	LVL	AGE	WHIP	ERA	DRA	WARP	MPH	FB%	WHF	CSP
2016	PEO	A	20	1.36	4.08	3.09	2.1				
2016	PMB	A+	20	1.21	3.62	2.78	1.0				
2017	SFD	AA	21	1.43	4.31	4.95	0.3				
2017	SLN	MLB	21	1.80	4.32	6.58	-0.1	100.6	66.5	16.8	44.3
2018	JUP	A+	22	1.32	3.97	6.50	-0.2				
2018	NWO	AAA	22	1.25	3.89	4.08	1.9				
2018	MIA	MLB	22	1.41	3.44	5.57	-0.1	97.9	60	11.8	45.2
2019	MIA	MLB	23	1.33	4.21	4.74	0.3	98.2	63.3	13.2	46.4

Sandy Alcantara, continued

Pitch Shape vs LHH

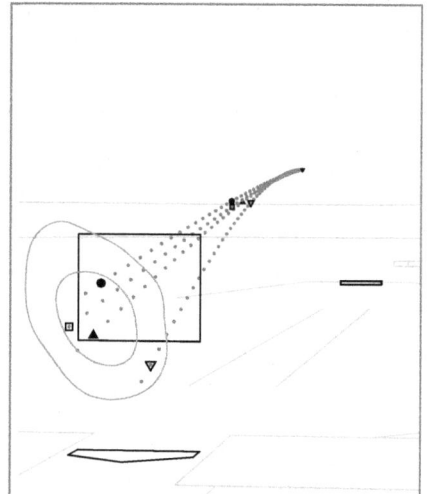

Pitch Shape vs RHH

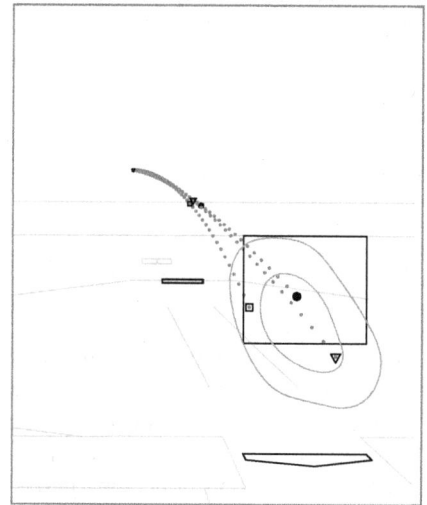

Type	Frequency	Velocity	H Movement	V Movement
● Fastball	33.5%	96.1 [111]	-6.6 [100]	-13.8 [106]
☐ Sinker	26.5%	95.8 [117]	-14.1 [87]	-20.7 [99]
+ Cutter				
▲ Changeup	13.2%	89.7 [117]	-12.6 [93]	-26.7 [102]
✕ Splitter				
▽ Slider	22.2%	86 [107]	4.1 [97]	-31.7 [104]
◇ Curveball	4.6%	82.1 [113]	4.1 [84]	-40.1 [118]
⊕ Slow Curveball				
✳ Knuckleball				
▼ Screwball				

Austin Brice   RHP

Born: 06/19/92   Age: 27   Bats: R   Throws: R
Height: 6'4"   Weight: 235   Origin: Round 9, 2010 Draft (#287 overall)

YEAR	TEAM	LVL	AGE	W	L	SV	G	GS	IP	H	HR	BB/9	K/9	K	GB%	BABIP
2016	JAX	AA	24	4	7	2	27	13	93¹	79	5	2.8	7.6	79	47%	.280
2016	NWO	AAA	24	0	0	2	5	0	8²	3	1	1.0	10.4	10	59%	.125
2016	MIA	MLB	24	0	1	0	15	0	14	9	2	3.2	9.0	14	53%	.194
2017	LOU	AAA	25	1	2	1	15	0	21¹	23	0	3.8	8.9	21	46%	.365
2017	CIN	MLB	25	0	0	0	22	0	32²	33	6	1.9	7.2	26	50%	.284
2018	CIN	MLB	26	2	3	0	33	0	37¹	39	9	3.1	7.7	32	53%	.286
2018	LOU	AAA	26	3	1	1	17	0	23¹	18	2	2.7	9.3	24	36%	.296
2019	MIA	MLB	27	0	1	0	11	0	11	10	1	3.7	8.6	11	45%	.291

Breakout: 19%   Improve: 28%   Collapse: 19%   Attrition: 34%   MLB: 64%
Comparables: Adam Ottavino, J.D. Martin, Kyle Lobstein

A decade ago, we almost certainly would have heard from the sabermetric community that Brice didn't deserve his poor ERA. His walks and strikeouts were acceptable, and he even managed to keep the ball on the ground at a strong clip. There would have been a lot of xFIP talk thrown around. Fortunately, we have better tools now. The main issue is something that seemed to plague many Reds pitchers: he can't help but give up the long ball. He was better across the board in Triple-A.

YEAR	TEAM	LVL	AGE	WHIP	ERA	DRA	WARP	MPH	FB%	WHF	CSP
2016	JAX	AA	24	1.16	2.89	3.15	2.1				
2016	NWO	AAA	24	0.46	1.04	1.86	0.3				
2016	MIA	MLB	24	1.00	7.07	4.60	0.1	96.6	66.3	12.4	47.1
2017	LOU	AAA	25	1.50	3.80	3.88	0.3				
2017	CIN	MLB	25	1.22	4.96	4.76	0.2	95.6	62.4	11.9	51.1
2018	CIN	MLB	26	1.39	5.79	5.75	-0.4	95.4	68.4	10	50.1
2018	LOU	AAA	26	1.07	2.31	4.79	0.1				
2019	MIA	MLB	27	1.28	3.90	4.36	0.1	95.1	66.8	11.1	50.3

Austin Brice, continued

Pitch Shape vs LHH

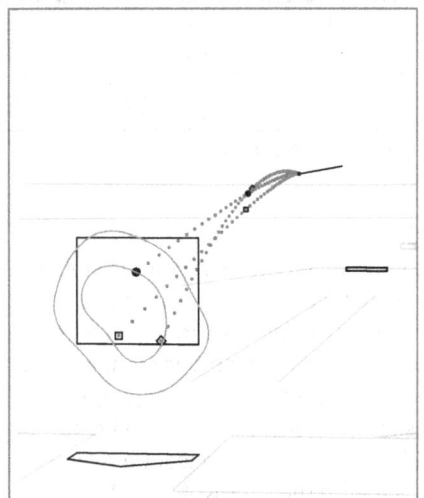

Pitch Shape vs RHH

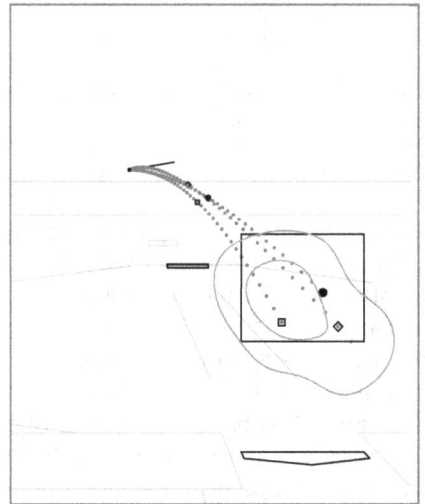

Type	Frequency	Velocity	H Movement	V Movement
● Fastball	20.8%	94.8 [107]	-9.3 [88]	-17.4 [95]
☐ Sinker	47.6%	94.5 [110]	-14.2 [87]	-25.1 [84]
+ Cutter				
▲ Changeup	2.0%	87.2 [108]	-8.9 [112]	-30.6 [90]
× Splitter				
▽ Slider	4.8%	85 [103]	5.3 [102]	-35.2 [94]
◇ Curveball	24.8%	83.1 [117]	7.6 [99]	-38.4 [122]
⊕ Slow Curveball				
✳ Knuckleball				
▼ Screwball				

Marlins Player Analysis - 47

Wei-Yin Chen LHP

Born: 07/21/85 Age: 33 Bats: R Throws: L
Height: 6'0" Weight: 200 Origin: International Free Agent, 2012

YEAR	TEAM	LVL	AGE	W	L	SV	G	GS	IP	H	HR	BB/9	K/9	K	GB%	BABIP
2016	MIA	MLB	30	5	5	0	22	22	123^1	134	22	1.8	7.3	100	42%	.302
2017	MIA	MLB	31	2	1	0	9	5	33	25	3	2.5	6.8	25	39%	.234
2018	MIA	MLB	32	6	12	0	26	26	133^1	131	19	3.2	7.5	111	38%	.285
2019	MIA	MLB	33	8	12	0	28	28	159	155	23	2.8	7.6	135	40%	.286

Breakout: 25% Improve: 49% Collapse: 19% Attrition: 9% MLB: 88%
Comparables: Ricky Nolasco, Aaron Harang, Kyle Lohse

It's hard to tell what's more noteworthy: Chen's ability to escape Tommy John surgery or his 2018 home/road splits. The veteran lefty who began the season a month late with left elbow inflammation, the latest in a string of arm injuries, had an average year with the Fish. Fans might have wanted him to pitch less on the road, where he owned a whopping 9.27 ERA in 55 1/2 innings compared to a 1.62 mark in 78 innings at Marlins Park. Chen tweaked his repertoire, opting to decrease his fastball usage in favor of his slider, his best pitch, which he bumped up to nearly a quarter usage. With health, he should remain a league-average starter who helps anchor a poor rotation, but with the salary of a no.2. starter for the next two years.

YEAR	TEAM	LVL	AGE	WHIP	ERA	DRA	WARP	MPH	FB%	WHF	CSP
2016	MIA	MLB	30	1.28	4.96	3.88	2.1	93.5	60.4	10.1	49
2017	MIA	MLB	31	1.03	3.82	4.28	0.5	92.4	65	9.5	48.5
2018	MIA	MLB	32	1.34	4.79	4.88	0.7	93.1	55.9	9.2	49.1
2019	MIA	MLB	33	1.26	4.28	4.83	0.4	92.1	57.6	9.4	48.3

Wei-Yin Chen, continued

Pitch Shape vs LHH

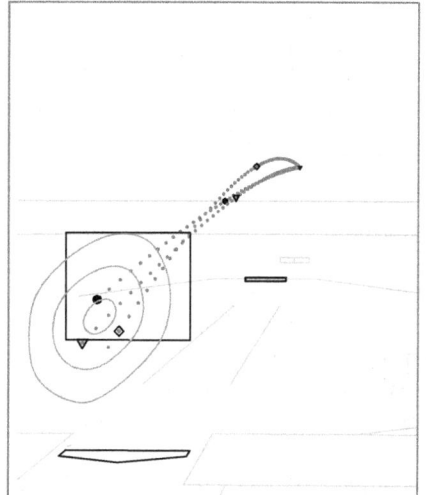

Pitch Shape vs RHH

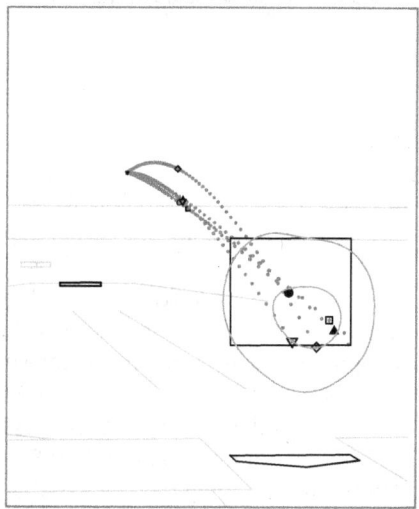

Type	Frequency	Velocity	H Movement	V Movement
● Fastball	53.2%	91.6 [97]	5.5 [106]	-14 [105]
☐ Sinker	2.7%	91.1 [93]	12.8 [99]	-18.1 [107]
+ Cutter				
▲ Changeup	11.8%	83.4 [92]	9.3 [110]	-25 [107]
✕ Splitter				
▽ Slider	22.0%	85.3 [104]	-4 [96]	-27.4 [117]
◇ Curveball	10.2%	73.7 [82]	-4.9 [88]	-54.3 [86]
⊕ Slow Curveball				
✳ Knuckleball				
▼ Screwball				

Miami Marlins 2019

Adam Conley LHP
Born: 05/24/90 Age: 29 Bats: L Throws: L
Height: 6'3" Weight: 200 Origin: Round 2, 2011 Draft (#72 overall)

YEAR	TEAM	LVL	AGE	W	L	SV	G	GS	IP	H	HR	BB/9	K/9	K	GB%	BABIP
2016	MIA	MLB	26	8	6	0	25	25	133^1	125	13	4.2	8.4	124	41%	.300
2017	NWO	AAA	27	3	3	0	12	12	62^1	69	7	3.6	5.9	41	39%	.310
2017	MIA	MLB	27	8	8	0	22	20	102^2	114	19	3.7	6.3	72	42%	.295
2018	NWO	AAA	28	2	4	0	8	8	40	45	6	3.2	5.6	25	50%	.300
2018	MIA	MLB	28	3	4	3	52	0	50^2	37	5	3.2	8.9	50	45%	.250
2019	MIA	MLB	29	3	3	8	54	0	57	50	6	3.8	8.2	52	43%	.283

Breakout: 30%   Improve: 45%   Collapse: 18%   Attrition: 23%   MLB: 76%
Comparables: Brian Duensing, Josh Outman, Jeff Niemann

After coming to terms with the fact that Conley was a bad starter, the Marlins shifted him to the bullpen where his fastball went from 90 mph to a whopping 96 mph. He also dropped his release point and turned to his changeup a little more than before. As you might expect, his strikeout rate jumped, he limited home runs and he allowed much less hard contact. A couple of unfortunate second-half outings ballooned his ERA, but Conley's turned himself into an effective multi-inning reliever capable of some high-leverage work as well. As the game shifts toward a heavier reliance on bullpens, Conley's role is sure to prove vital.

YEAR	TEAM	LVL	AGE	WHIP	ERA	DRA	WARP	MPH	FB%	WHF	CSP
2016	MIA	MLB	26	1.40	3.85	5.05	0.5	94.3	65.5	10.9	46
2017	NWO	AAA	27	1.51	5.49	4.49	0.8				
2017	MIA	MLB	27	1.52	6.14	6.64	-1.2	91.9	64.4	10.6	47.7
2018	NWO	AAA	28	1.48	5.18	4.29	0.6				
2018	MIA	MLB	28	1.09	4.09	3.58	0.8	97.3	56.9	15.6	46.9
2019	MIA	MLB	29	1.29	3.98	4.42	0.3	93.4	63.1	11.8	46.9

Adam Conley, continued

Pitch Shape vs LHH

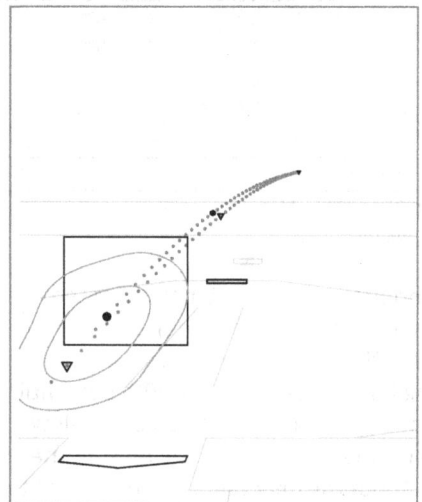

Pitch Shape vs RHH

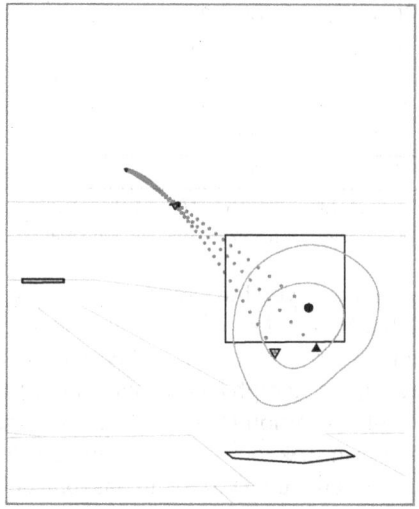

Type	Frequency	Velocity	H Movement	V Movement
● Fastball	56.8%	95.7 [110]	15.1 [61]	-15.9 [100]
□ Sinker				
+ Cutter				
▲ Changeup	27.0%	86.3 [104]	15.5 [77]	-25.3 [106]
✕ Splitter				
▽ Slider	16.1%	88.6 [118]	-0.2 [80]	-25.1 [124]
◇ Curveball				
⬗ Slow Curveball				
✲ Knuckleball				
▼ Screwball				

Marlins Player Analysis - 51

Miami Marlins 2019

Jarlin Garcia LHP
Born: 01/18/93 Age: 26 Bats: L Throws: L
Height: 6'3" Weight: 215 Origin: International Free Agent, 2010

YEAR	TEAM	LVL	AGE	W	L	SV	G	GS	IP	H	HR	BB/9	K/9	K	GB%	BABIP
2016	JAX	AA	23	1	3	0	9	9	39²	38	4	2.5	6.1	27	48%	.274
2016	JUP	A+	23	0	0	0	5	0	7	4	1	1.3	6.4	5	48%	.150
2017	MIA	MLB	24	1	2	0	68	0	53¹	47	6	2.9	7.1	42	41%	.263
2018	NWO	AAA	25	2	2	0	10	9	48²	57	5	2.6	6.1	33	40%	.323
2018	MIA	MLB	25	3	3	0	29	7	66	59	16	3.8	5.5	40	44%	.222
2019	MIA	MLB	26	3	4	0	46	3	61	62	8	3.5	6.8	47	42%	.287

Breakout: 23% Improve: 37% Collapse: 20% Attrition: 27% MLB: 63%
Comparables: Zach Stewart, Brandon Workman, Liam Hendriks

Sometimes you have to search deep to understand why a pitcher regressed. Other times, like in Garcia's case last season, you just have to look at his velocity. The southpaw lost two ticks across the board, leaving his fastball averaging 92 mph last season, and putting him right around the 50th percentile in velocity among lefty peers. Add a loss of control and he set new career-low marks in strikeout rate and walk rate. Even worse, he allowed the most home runs of any relief pitcher in baseball (16). About the only value he provides at the moment is name value, as the organization finally has someone whose name rhymes with the mascot.

YEAR	TEAM	LVL	AGE	WHIP	ERA	DRA	WARP	MPH	FB%	WHF	CSP
2016	JAX	AA	23	1.24	4.54	3.19	0.9				
2016	JUP	A+	23	0.71	1.29	3.42	0.1				
2017	MIA	MLB	24	1.20	4.72	4.42	0.4	95.8	49.8	12.1	47.8
2018	NWO	AAA	25	1.46	4.81	4.06	0.8				
2018	MIA	MLB	25	1.32	4.91	5.51	-0.3	93.9	52.5	8.4	49.3
2019	MIA	MLB	26	1.38	4.87	5.18	-0.2	94.3	52.3	10.1	49.5

Jarlin Garcia, continued

Pitch Shape vs LHH

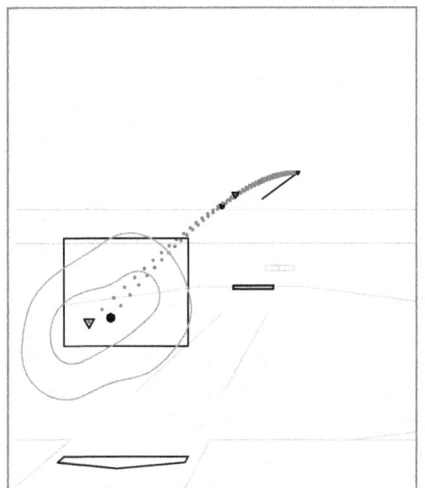

Pitch Shape vs RHH

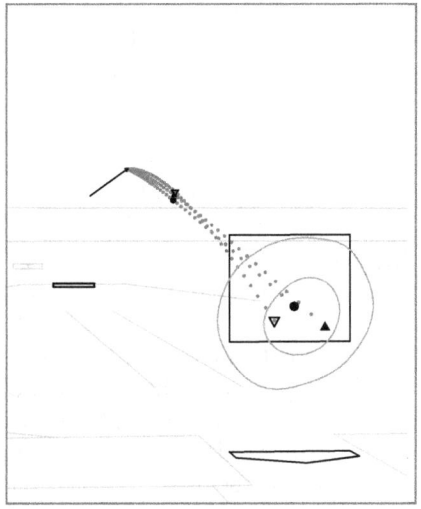

Type	Frequency	Velocity	H Movement	V Movement
● Fastball	52.5%	92.7 [101]	13.2 [70]	-18.3 [92]
☐ Sinker				
+ Cutter				
▲ Changeup	24.9%	86.3 [104]	16.9 [70]	-26.6 [102]
✕ Splitter				
▽ Slider	22.6%	85.6 [105]	-2.6 [90]	-28.1 [114]
◇ Curveball				
⬥ Slow Curveball				
✱ Knuckleball				
▼ Screwball				

Tayron Guerrero RHP

Born: 01/09/91 Age: 28 Bats: R Throws: R
Height: 6'8" Weight: 210 Origin: International Free Agent, 2009

YEAR	TEAM	LVL	AGE	W	L	SV	G	GS	IP	H	HR	BB/9	K/9	K	GB%	BABIP
2016	SDN	MLB	25	0	0	0	1	0	2	3	0	4.5	0.0	0	50%	.375
2016	ELP	AAA	25	0	0	0	13	0	12	12	2	6.8	8.2	11	43%	.286
2016	SAN	AA	25	0	3	0	19	0	23²	20	2	3.8	9.5	25	48%	.300
2016	JAX	AA	25	1	1	4	12	0	14	11	0	1.9	9.6	15	27%	.297
2017	JAX	AA	26	0	1	0	17	0	16	14	3	7.9	12.4	22	41%	.306
2017	NWO	AAA	26	3	2	0	13	0	15¹	12	2	7.0	6.5	11	44%	.217
2018	MIA	MLB	27	1	3	0	60	0	58	64	8	4.7	10.6	68	45%	.354
2019	MIA	MLB	28	3	3	4	54	0	57	51	7	4.6	9.3	59	42%	.289

Breakout: 13% Improve: 25% Collapse: 15% Attrition: 21% MLB: 47%
Comparables: Royce Ring, Brandon Cunniff, Cody Eppley

Guerrero burst onto the scenes on Opening Day against the Cubs, striking out his first four batters of the year. People wondered who the hell this 6-foot-8 dude averaging nearly 99 mph on his fastball was. Guerrero at times showed an above-average slider to pair with his heater, but he was very inconsistent in the zone, giving up too many free passes and ranking in the bottom five of reliever first-pitch strikes. Pair that with the fourth-worst BABIP in his class and it's easy to understand why just throwing a million miles an hour didn't work for him.

YEAR	TEAM	LVL	AGE	WHIP	ERA	DRA	WARP	MPH	FB%	WHF	CSP
2016	SDN	MLB	25	2.00	4.50	6.75	0.0	96.2	86.4	0	39.5
2016	ELP	AAA	25	1.75	6.00	4.84	0.0				
2016	SAN	AA	25	1.27	4.94	3.74	0.3				
2016	JAX	AA	25	1.00	1.93	2.51	0.4				
2017	JAX	AA	26	1.75	3.38	5.98	-0.2				
2017	NWO	AAA	26	1.57	5.87	4.47	0.1				
2018	MIA	MLB	27	1.62	5.43	4.80	0.1	101.5	79.2	12.4	49.4
2019	MIA	MLB	28	1.41	4.58	4.91	-0.1	100.8	79.7	12.3	46

Tayron Guerrero, continued

Pitch Shape vs LHH

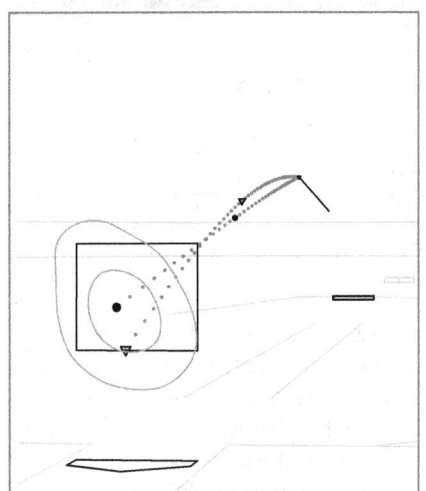

Pitch Shape vs RHH

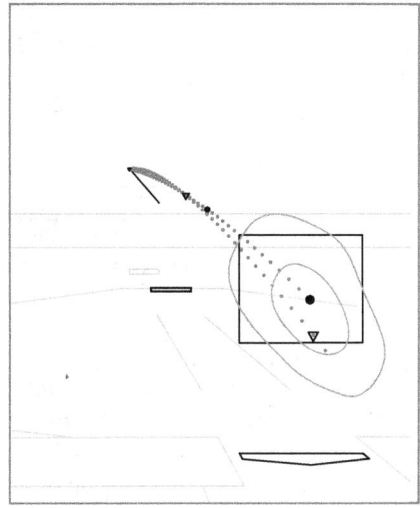

Type	Frequency	Velocity	H Movement	V Movement
● Fastball	79.2%	99.4 [122]	-8.7 [91]	-11.5 [113]
☐ Sinker				
+ Cutter				
▲ Changeup	1.6%	94.2 [135]	-10.9 [102]	-19.2 [124]
✕ Splitter				
▽ Slider	19.2%	86.5 [109]	3.8 [96]	-32.4 [102]
◇ Curveball				
⊕ Slow Curveball				
✱ Knuckleball				
▼ Screwball				

Trevor Richards RHP

Born: 05/15/93 Age: 26 Bats: R Throws: R
Height: 6'2" Weight: 190 Origin: Undrafted Free Agent, 2016

YEAR	TEAM	LVL	AGE	W	L	SV	G	GS	IP	H	HR	BB/9	K/9	K	GB%	BABIP
2016	BAT	A-	23	0	0	0	3	1	10^2	9	1	1.7	12.7	15	28%	.333
2016	GRB	A	23	2	3	0	8	8	43^2	29	3	2.9	7.8	38	47%	.222
2017	JUP	A+	24	7	4	0	13	11	70^2	54	2	1.5	10.3	81	62%	.284
2017	JAX	AA	24	5	7	0	14	14	75^1	67	4	2.2	9.2	77	50%	.297
2018	NWO	AAA	25	3	2	0	6	6	39^1	31	4	0.9	8.5	37	50%	.260
2018	MIA	MLB	25	4	9	0	25	25	126^1	121	15	3.8	9.3	130	38%	.309
2019	MIA	MLB	26	6	10	0	24	24	127	118	17	3.2	8.9	126	42%	.289

Breakout: 31% Improve: 53% Collapse: 18% Attrition: 19% MLB: 93%
Comparables: Marc Rzepczynski, Angel Guzman, Anthony DeSclafani

There can't be a Trevor Richards blurb without immediately mentioning his double-plus changeup that ranks as one of the best in baseball. It's an elite circle-change that he wields with aplomb, using it to rack up the 11th-best whiffs-per-swing rate among his peers thanks to its massive tumble. However, he neutralized that weapon by pairing it with one of the worst fastballs in baseball, a really hittable 91 mph offering that was below the 20th percentile in whiffs per swing. Overall, it was a solid rookie campaign for someone once seen as organizational depth. Richards is a good complement in the back end of a rotation.

YEAR	TEAM	LVL	AGE	WHIP	ERA	DRA	WARP	MPH	FB%	WHF	CSP
2016	BAT	A-	23	1.03	1.69	1.26	0.5				
2016	GRB	A	23	0.98	2.68	3.44	0.8				
2017	JUP	A+	24	0.93	2.17	2.94	1.9				
2017	JAX	AA	24	1.13	2.87	2.93	2.0				
2018	NWO	AAA	25	0.89	2.06	2.64	1.3				
2018	MIA	MLB	25	1.39	4.42	3.57	2.5	92.2	54.8	11.7	44.4
2019	MIA	MLB	26	1.26	4.07	4.59	0.7	91.8	55.8	12	45.2

Trevor Richards, continued

Pitch Shape vs LHH

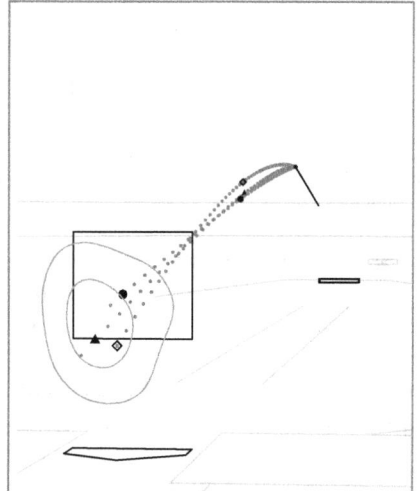

Pitch Shape vs RHH

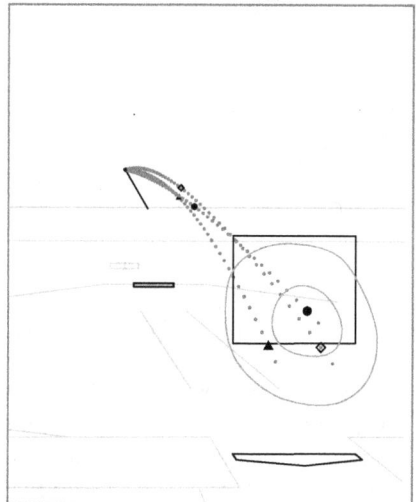

Type	Frequency	Velocity	H Movement	V Movement
● Fastball	54.8%	91.3 [96]	-7 [99]	-14.4 [104]
☐ Sinker				
+ Cutter				
▲ Changeup	32.3%	83.4 [92]	-12.8 [92]	-29.9 [92]
✕ Splitter				
▽ Slider				
◇ Curveball	12.9%	81 [109]	2.1 [76]	-40.2 [118]
✪ Slow Curveball				
✳ Knuckleball				
▼ Screwball				

Miami Marlins 2019

Sergio Romo   RHP
Born: 03/04/83   Age: 36   Bats: R   Throws: R
Height: 5'11"   Weight: 185   Origin: Round 28, 2005 Draft (#852 overall)

YEAR	TEAM	LVL	AGE	W	L	SV	G	GS	IP	H	HR	BB/9	K/9	K	GB%	BABIP
2016	SFN	MLB	33	1	0	4	40	0	30^2	26	5	2.1	9.7	33	39%	.292
2017	LAN	MLB	34	1	1	0	30	0	25	23	7	4.3	11.2	31	35%	.276
2017	TBA	MLB	34	2	0	0	25	0	30^2	19	2	2.1	8.2	28	40%	.218
2018	TBA	MLB	35	3	4	25	73	5	67^1	65	11	2.7	10.0	75	38%	.309
2019	MIA	MLB	36	3	3	0	54	0	57	52	8	3.4	9.2	59	39%	.287

Breakout: 24%   Improve: 45%   Collapse: 16%   Attrition: 6%   MLB: 76%
Comparables: Kyle Farnsworth, Lee Smith, Francisco Rodriguez

Prior to May 19, 2018, Romo had made all 588 of his major-league appearances as a reliever. He made his first start that day. He made his second the next day. Romo became the first pitcher in over a century to start a game, have a 1-2-3 inning and come out right after. He would start five games on the year before the Rays traded Alex Colome and Romo returned to a familiar role late in games. He collected 25 saves while going from opener to closer and was generally effective as the pen's elder statesman. Romo's fiery personality does not match his mid-80s fastball, but his eccentricity is matched by the quirkiness of his slider with disco-era velocity. He threw the slider nearly 60 percent of the time, and while it may have lost a little bite from his peak, it was still a steady source of outs. Under six feet tall and on the wrong side of 35, Romo continues to defy the odds with flair. In addition to his cameo in the "rotation" he also appeared at third base and almost fought Aaron Judge. Tune in next season to see what new tricks the old dog can pull off.

YEAR	TEAM	LVL	AGE	WHIP	ERA	DRA	WARP	MPH	FB%	WHF	CSP
2016	SFN	MLB	33	1.08	2.64	2.45	0.9	87.8	32	15.7	42.4
2017	LAN	MLB	34	1.40	6.12	2.58	0.7	87.9	27.2	15.4	41.1
2017	TBA	MLB	34	0.85	1.47	3.76	0.5	87.4	41.5	16.3	41.7
2018	TBA	MLB	35	1.26	4.14	2.80	1.7	87.7	30.1	14.6	44
2019	MIA	MLB	36	1.27	4.33	4.71	0.1	86.5	31.1	14.9	41.9

Sergio Romo, continued

Pitch Shape vs LHH	Pitch Shape vs RHH
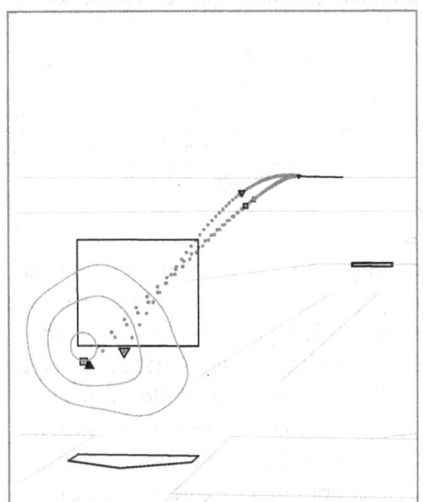	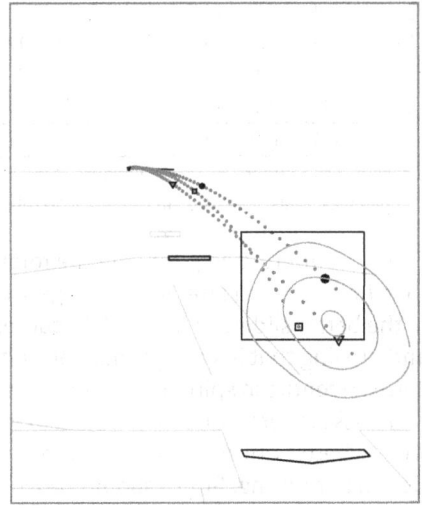

Type	Frequency	Velocity	H Movement	V Movement
● Fastball	13.8%	87.2 [83]	-10.4 [83]	-21.2 [83]
□ Sinker	16.3%	86.6 [71]	-15.7 [75]	-30.6 [66]
+ Cutter				
▲ Changeup	11.8%	81.1 [83]	-16.3 [73]	-34 [80]
× Splitter				
▽ Slider	58.1%	77.5 [69]	14.3 [141]	-35.2 [93]
◇ Curveball				
✦ Slow Curveball				
✱ Knuckleball				
▼ Screwball				

Miami Marlins 2019

Caleb Smith LHP

Born: 07/28/91   Age: 27   Bats: R   Throws: L
Height: 6'2"   Weight: 205   Origin: Round 14, 2013 Draft (#434 overall)

YEAR	TEAM	LVL	AGE	W	L	SV	G	GS	IP	H	HR	BB/9	K/9	K	GB%	BABIP
2016	TRN	AA	24	3	5	3	27	7	63^2	66	4	2.8	9.9	70	45%	.344
2017	SWB	AAA	25	9	1	0	18	17	98	75	7	2.6	8.9	97	42%	.264
2017	NYA	MLB	25	0	1	0	9	2	18^2	21	4	4.8	8.7	18	28%	.315
2018	MIA	MLB	26	5	6	0	16	16	77^1	63	10	3.8	10.2	88	31%	.276
2019	MIA	MLB	27	3	5	0	13	13	65	58	9	3.2	9.6	69	37%	.289

Breakout: 21%   Improve: 38%   Collapse: 17%   Attrition: 25%   MLB: 74%
Comparables: Mark Leiter, Dustin Nippert, Kyle Lobstein

The most interesting pitcher in the rotation might be one who pitched for less than half a season after left lat surgery cut his year short in June. Smith rode one of the better sliders in baseball to success, neutralizing both righties and lefties and proving that it's a legitimate out-pitch. His fastball, which finished in the top 20th percentile in spin rate, elevates his mediocre changeup. While the swing and miss is there, concerns remain over his ability to command his pitches, as well as better utilize a changeup that was little more than a show-me offering. Health permitting, Smith should be a decent sleeper in a forgotten rotation.

YEAR	TEAM	LVL	AGE	WHIP	ERA	DRA	WARP	MPH	FB%	WHF	CSP
2016	TRN	AA	24	1.35	3.96	3.04	1.4				
2017	SWB	AAA	25	1.05	2.39	4.04	1.8				
2017	NYA	MLB	25	1.66	7.71	4.92	0.1	95.5	50.3	14.4	42.2
2018	MIA	MLB	26	1.24	4.19	4.05	1.1	94.3	59.1	13.3	48.7
2019	MIA	MLB	27	1.22	3.97	4.46	0.4	94.0	58.4	13.7	46.4

Caleb Smith, continued

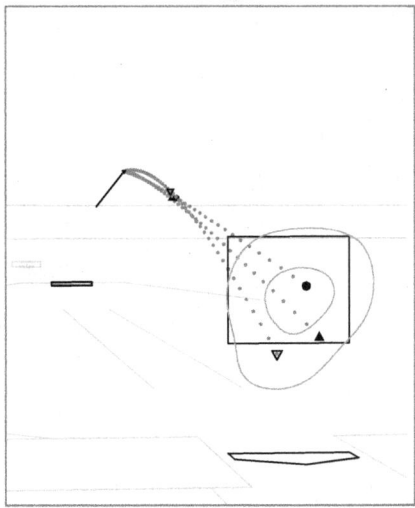

Type	Frequency	Velocity	H Movement	V Movement
● Fastball	59.1%	93.2 [102]	11.7 [77]	-13.9 [106]
☐ Sinker				
+ Cutter				
▲ Changeup	13.7%	84.5 [97]	13.9 [86]	-25.9 [104]
✕ Splitter				
▽ Slider	27.2%	82.1 [90]	-2 [88]	-38.3 [84]
◇ Curveball				
✦ Slow Curveball				
✳ Knuckleball				
▼ Screwball				

Drew Steckenrider RHP

Born: 01/10/91 Age: 28 Bats: R Throws: R
Height: 6'5" Weight: 215 Origin: Round 8, 2012 Draft (#257 overall)

YEAR	TEAM	LVL	AGE	W	L	SV	G	GS	IP	H	HR	BB/9	K/9	K	GB%	BABIP
2016	JUP	A+	25	0	0	1	6	0	10	2	0	1.8	15.3	17	64%	.143
2016	JAX	AA	25	1	0	6	24	0	30^1	12	0	3.0	11.6	39	54%	.197
2016	NWO	AAA	25	0	1	7	10	0	11^2	11	1	5.4	11.6	15	52%	.333
2017	NWO	AAA	26	0	1	5	26	0	33^1	18	3	2.2	11.9	44	43%	.217
2017	MIA	MLB	26	1	1	1	37	0	34^2	30	4	4.7	14.0	54	43%	.347
2018	MIA	MLB	27	4	4	5	71	0	64^2	55	7	3.8	10.3	74	34%	.296
2019	MIA	MLB	28	3	3	20	59	0	62	54	8	4.1	10.4	72	41%	.291

Breakout: 23% Improve: 37% Collapse: 26% Attrition: 16% MLB: 74%
Comparables: Michael Wuertz, Jerry Blevins, Zach Putnam

Steckenrider took a step backward from an impressive rookie campaign in which he punched out nearly 36 percent of batters faced. While his 27 percent mark in 2018 is nothing to scoff at, his peripherals deteriorated and he turned into an extreme fly-ball pitcher after ditching his slider for a cutter. The whiffs remained the same on his new pitch, so it's not to blame for his loss of strikeouts. Instead, heatmaps showed he didn't elevate his fastball last year as much as in 2017, likely leading to the drop in whiff rate on his primary pitch. He improved his walk rate from bad to manageable, and he could be a candidate to close thanks to his raw stuff.

YEAR	TEAM	LVL	AGE	WHIP	ERA	DRA	WARP	MPH	FB%	WHF	CSP
2016	JUP	A+	25	0.40	0.00	2.00	0.4				
2016	JAX	AA	25	0.73	1.48	1.65	1.1				
2016	NWO	AAA	25	1.54	5.40	2.96	0.3				
2017	NWO	AAA	26	0.78	1.62	1.67	1.3				
2017	MIA	MLB	26	1.38	2.34	3.70	0.6	96.8	77.8	14.8	49.9
2018	MIA	MLB	27	1.27	3.90	4.44	0.4	96.4	76.4	12.2	50.8
2019	MIA	MLB	28	1.32	3.99	4.43	0.3	95.9	77.3	13.1	50.7

Drew Steckenrider, continued

Pitch Shape vs LHH

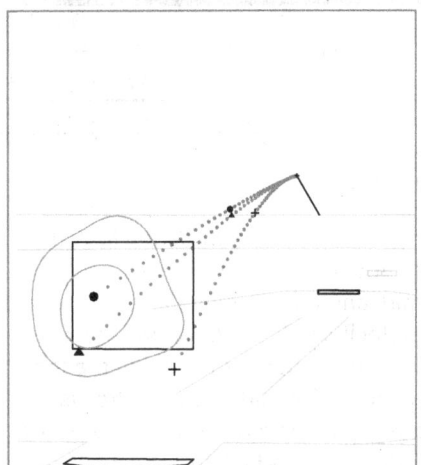

Pitch Shape vs RHH

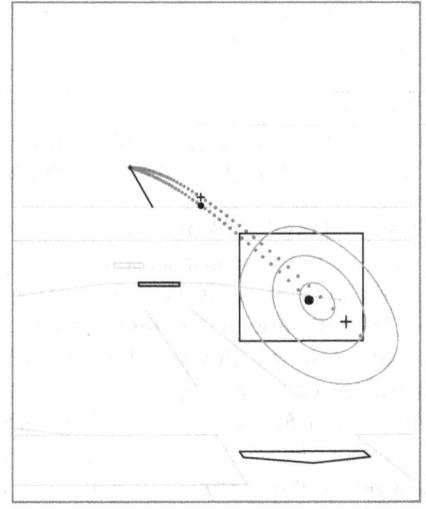

Type	Frequency	Velocity	H Movement	V Movement
● Fastball	76.4%	95.1 [108]	-7.7 [95]	-10.8 [116]
☐ Sinker				
+ Cutter	15.9%	88.5 [98]	2.7 [105]	-26.5 [89]
▲ Changeup	3.6%	89.4 [116]	-10.4 [104]	-22.2 [115]
✕ Splitter				
▽ Slider	4.1%	83.1 [94]	0.3 [80]	-38.7 [83]
◇ Curveball				
⬥ Slow Curveball				
✳ Knuckleball				
▼ Screwball				

Dan Straily RHP

Born: 12/01/88 Age: 30 Bats: R Throws: R
Height: 6'2" Weight: 220 Origin: Round 24, 2009 Draft (#723 overall)

YEAR	TEAM	LVL	AGE	W	L	SV	G	GS	IP	H	HR	BB/9	K/9	K	GB%	BABIP
2016	CIN	MLB	27	14	8	0	34	31	191[1]	154	31	3.4	7.6	162	34%	.239
2017	MIA	MLB	28	10	9	0	33	33	181[2]	176	31	3.0	8.4	170	36%	.288
2018	MIA	MLB	29	5	6	0	23	23	122[1]	107	20	3.8	7.3	99	34%	.256
2019	MIA	MLB	30	6	11	0	26	26	137	130	20	3.4	8.1	123	36%	.282

Breakout: 18% Improve: 35% Collapse: 17% Attrition: 17% MLB: 71%
Comparables: Byung-Hyun Kim, Scott Richmond, Jason Bergmann

Straily led the 2017 Marlins in starts, but right forearm inflammation forced him to miss a month of last season. Whether or not he felt the side effects of that as the season wore on is more speculation than anything, but overall he regressed. His fastball, though it maintained similar velocity, induced fewer swings, and he began pitching it closer to the center of the zone rather than favoring the top like in the past. Throwing a 90 mph fastball down the middle more often is how you allow a .553 slugging on the pitch. Straily quietly has one of the more elite changeups in baseball, ranking in the top 15 in ground-ball rate and whiff rates last year, but he opted to turn more to his slider, enough that in his final start of the year he threw it more than his heater. It's an average pitch, but not one to prioritize. Still just 30 and under team control for two more seasons, Straily can be counted on to be an innings eater, but he's trending closer to the back of a rotation than the middle.

YEAR	TEAM	LVL	AGE	WHIP	ERA	DRA	WARP	MPH	FB%	WHF	CSP
2016	CIN	MLB	27	1.19	3.76	4.76	1.3	91.8	51	11.1	47.4
2017	MIA	MLB	28	1.30	4.26	4.26	2.7	92.1	50.5	13.2	47.6
2018	MIA	MLB	29	1.30	4.12	5.19	0.2	91.9	49.3	11.2	46.5
2019	MIA	MLB	30	1.29	4.50	5.06	0.0	91.2	50.1	11.9	46.9

Dan Straily, continued

Pitch Shape vs LHH

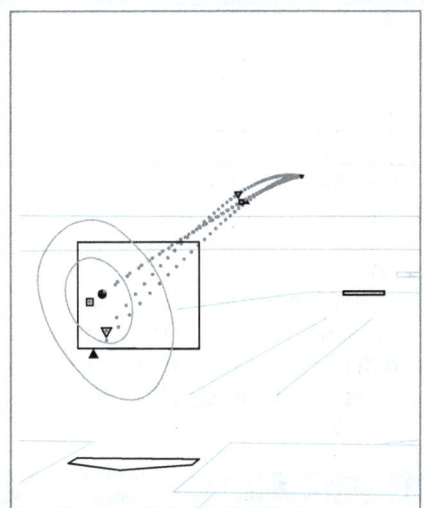

Pitch Shape vs RHH

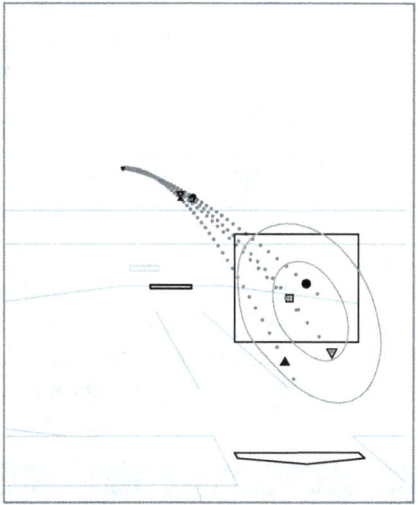

Type	Frequency	Velocity	H Movement	V Movement
● Fastball	43.6%	90.9 [95]	-6.9 [99]	-14.1 [105]
☐ Sinker	5.7%	90.9 [92]	-12 [105]	-17.3 [110]
+ Cutter				
▲ Changeup	17.0%	84.1 [95]	-10.3 [105]	-32.3 [85]
✕ Splitter				
▽ Slider	32.9%	84.2 [99]	5.1 [101]	-32.2 [102]
◇ Curveball	0.7%	75.4 [89]	7.4 [98]	-49.4 [97]
✥ Slow Curveball				
✳ Knuckleball				
▼ Screwball				

Miami Marlins 2019

Jose Urena RHP
Born: 09/12/91   Age: 27   Bats: R   Throws: R
Height: 6'2"   Weight: 200   Origin: International Free Agent, 2008

YEAR	TEAM	LVL	AGE	W	L	SV	G	GS	IP	H	HR	BB/9	K/9	K	GB%	BABIP
2016	NWO	AAA	24	3	3	0	12	12	48^1	41	4	3.9	7.6	41	46%	.278
2016	MIA	MLB	24	4	9	1	28	12	83^2	91	11	3.1	6.2	58	49%	.297
2017	MIA	MLB	25	14	7	0	34	28	169^2	152	26	3.4	6.0	113	44%	.249
2018	MIA	MLB	26	9	12	0	31	31	174	155	19	2.6	6.7	130	51%	.272
2019	MIA	MLB	27	8	11	0	27	27	153	140	16	3.1	7.5	128	47%	.283

Breakout: 14%   Improve: 34%   Collapse: 22%   Attrition: 18%   MLB: 78%
Comparables: Nick Martinez, Kendall Graveman, Chris Tillman

Urena is a proud, card-carrying member of the Throw Hard, Strike No One Out club. Behind a fastball that averaged more than 96 mph, the righty posted yet another strikeout rate below 20 percent in 2018. He used one of those fastballs to hit Ronald Acuna Jr., who was on his leadoff home run tear in mid-August. His primarily value is eating innings at this point, as not much else about his game has the potential be above average.

YEAR	TEAM	LVL	AGE	WHIP	ERA	DRA	WARP	MPH	FB%	WHF	CSP
2016	NWO	AAA	24	1.28	3.17	3.36	1.1				
2016	MIA	MLB	24	1.43	6.13	5.75	-0.5	97.7	66.2	10	43.1
2017	MIA	MLB	25	1.27	3.82	5.25	0.5	97.3	56.2	9.1	45.2
2018	MIA	MLB	26	1.18	3.98	4.01	2.6	97.5	58.8	9.7	46.2
2019	MIA	MLB	27	1.23	4.00	4.51	1.0	97.0	59.6	9.6	45.6

Jose Urena, continued

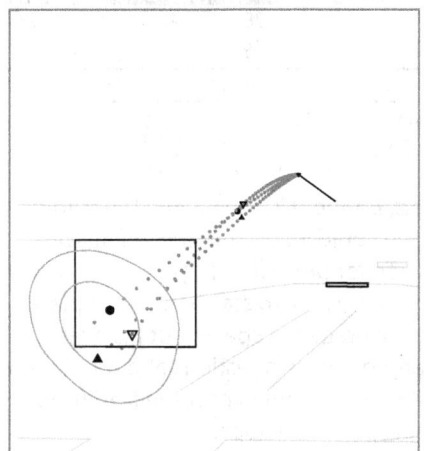
Pitch Shape vs LHH

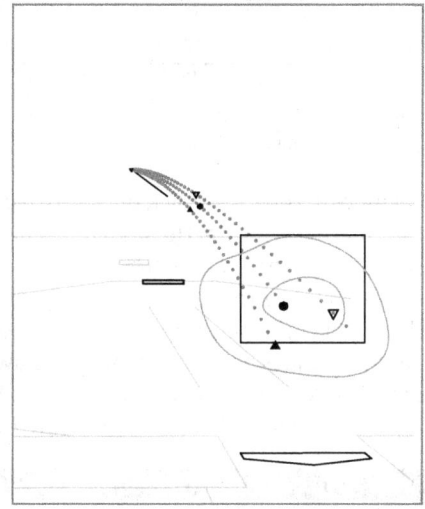
Pitch Shape vs RHH

Type	Frequency	Velocity	H Movement	V Movement
● Fastball	58.8%	96.2 [112]	-13.1 [70]	-16.8 [97]
☐ Sinker				
+ Cutter				
▲ Changeup	18.4%	90.2 [120]	-12.6 [93]	-20.9 [119]
✕ Splitter				
▽ Slider	22.7%	86.7 [110]	1.3 [84]	-26.1 [120]
◇ Curveball				
⊕ Slow Curveball				
✷ Knuckleball				
▼ Screwball				

Miami Marlins 2019

Will Banfield C
Born: 11/18/99 Age: 19 Bats: R Throws: R
Height: 6'0" Weight: 200 Origin: Round 2, 2018 Draft (#69 overall)

YEAR	TEAM	LVL	AGE	PA	R	2B	3B	HR	RBI	BB	K	SB	CS	AVG/OBP/SLG
2018	MRL	RK	18	94	7	8	1	0	14	7	28	0	1	.256/.330/.378
2018	GRB	A	18	52	5	0	0	3	4	4	15	0	0	.208/.269/.396
2019	MIA	MLB	19	251	16	5	0	6	22	6	94	0	0	.133/.154/.232

Breakout: 6% Improve: 8% Collapse: 0% Attrition: 4% MLB: 11%
Comparables: Francisco Pena, Nomar Mazara, Gleyber Torres

Taken with the nicest pick of the 2018 draft, Banfield is considered the Marlins' catcher of the future. He has everything you could want from the defensive spectrum: strong athleticism, the foundation for pitch-framing and a plus arm to nail runners. With that alone, Banfield is an easy pick to stay behind the plate. He exhibits plus raw power and has above-average bat speed, but his over-aggressiveness and lack of off-speed awareness raise questions about the future of the hit tool. He reached Low-A as an 18-year-old, but expect the Marlins to slow roll the rest of the way to ensure he properly develops.

YEAR	TEAM	LVL	AGE	PA	DRC+	VORP	BABIP	BRR	FRAA	WARP
2018	MRL	RK	18	94	81	1.8	.375	-0.9	C(22): 1.2	0.0
2018	GRB	A	18	52	77	0.7	.233	0.1	C(14): 0.1	0.0
2019	MIA	MLB	19	251	-6	-21.4	.180	-0.5	C 0	-2.3

Garrett Cooper LF

Born: 12/25/90   Age: 28   Bats: R   Throws: R
Height: 6'6"   Weight: 230   Origin: Round 6, 2013 Draft (#182 overall)

YEAR	TEAM	LVL	AGE	PA	R	2B	3B	HR	RBI	BB	K	SB	CS	AVG/OBP/SLG
2016	BLX	AA	25	329	27	22	1	4	49	20	55	3	3	.299/.350/.419
2016	CSP	AAA	25	139	17	5	0	5	20	10	20	0	0	.276/.331/.433
2017	CSP	AAA	26	320	64	29	0	17	82	33	48	0	0	.366/.428/.652
2017	NYA	MLB	26	45	3	5	1	0	6	1	12	0	0	.326/.333/.488
2018	MIA	MLB	27	38	2	1	0	0	2	4	12	0	0	.212/.316/.242
2019	MIA	MLB	28	209	20	8	1	5	22	16	46	0	0	.238/.301/.370

Breakout: 8%   Improve: 17%   Collapse: 8%   Attrition: 23%   MLB: 46%
Comparables: Russ Canzler, Jason Rogers, Jesus Guzman

Persistent right wrist injuries turned 2018 into a lost year for Cooper, who was aiming to become at worst a platoon bat for the Fish and at best the everyday first baseman after Justin Bour's departure. The 6-foot-6 lefty bat showcased a 1.080 OPS in Triple-A Colorado Springs while with the Brewers in 2017, along with a 10 percent walk rate and just a 15 percent strikeout rate. He has 83 not-very-great MLB at-bats to his name, but a promising profile that should net positive returns in 2019.

YEAR	TEAM	LVL	AGE	PA	DRC+	VORP	BABIP	BRR	FRAA	WARP
2016	BLX	AA	25	329	124	16.5	.351	-2.5	1B(59): -0.3, RF(16): 0.7	0.3
2016	CSP	AAA	25	139	105	-2.3	.291	0.1	1B(22): 0.1, LF(11): -1.1	0.0
2017	CSP	AAA	26	320	182	26.3	.386	-2.3	1B(73): 4.3	3.1
2017	NYA	MLB	26	45	80	1.3	.438	0.0	1B(13): 0.0	0.0
2018	MIA	MLB	27	38	67	0.3	.333	0.4	LF(6): 0.7, 1B(4): 1.1	0.1
2019	MIA	MLB	28	209	88	2.7	.282	-0.4	1B 0, LF 0	0.3

Jose Devers SS

Born: 12/07/99 Age: 19 Bats: L Throws: R
Height: 6'0" Weight: 155 Origin: International Free Agent, 2016

YEAR	TEAM	LVL	AGE	PA	R	2B	3B	HR	RBI	BB	K	SB	CS	AVG/OBP/SLG
2017	DYA	RK	17	47	4	2	1	0	7	0	16	1	0	.239/.255/.326
2017	YAN	RK	17	169	17	7	2	1	9	18	21	15	3	.246/.359/.348
2018	GRB	A	18	362	46	12	4	0	24	15	49	13	6	.273/.313/.332
2019	MIA	MLB	19	251	20	4	1	4	17	1	69	3	1	.166/.170/.237

Breakout: 4% Improve: 6% Collapse: 0% Attrition: 3% MLB: 7%
Comparables: Carlos Triunfel, Alcides Escobar, Elvis Andrus

Rafael Devers' cousin doesn't possess the same kind of pedigree or boom in his bat. Instead, Jose is a glove-first player likely to remain at shortstop thanks to smooth footwork, slick transfers and a good enough arm that should stave off a move to second base. Because he'll stick up the middle, his light offensive game is still good enough to carry the profile. He shows good bat-to-ball skills, solid pitch recognition that lowers his strikeouts and enough speed to take advantage on the basepaths. His linear stroke sucks any punch out of his bat because he mashes everything into the ground. Becoming an average big-league regular is within reach.

YEAR	TEAM	LVL	AGE	PA	DRC+	VORP	BABIP	BRR	FRAA	WARP
2017	DYA	RK	17	47	55	-2.5	.367	-0.7	SS(7): 0.2, 2B(3): -0.1	-0.2
2017	YAN	RK	17	169	123	10.4	.277	-2.9	SS(39): -0.4	0.2
2018	GRB	A	18	362	92	4.0	.318	-2.6	SS(59): 2.2, 2B(15): 0.0	0.2
2019	MIA	MLB	19	251	3	-20.0	.208	0.2	SS -1, 2B 0	-2.2

Isan Diaz 2B

Born: 05/27/96 Age: 23 Bats: L Throws: R
Height: 5'10" Weight: 185 Origin: Round 2, 2014 Draft (#70 overall)

YEAR	TEAM	LVL	AGE	PA	R	2B	3B	HR	RBI	BB	K	SB	CS	AVG/OBP/SLG
2016	WIS	A	20	587	71	34	5	20	75	72	148	11	8	.264/.358/.469
2017	CAR	A+	21	455	59	20	0	13	54	62	121	9	3	.222/.334/.376
2018	JAX	AA	22	356	44	19	1	10	42	53	95	10	3	.245/.365/.418
2018	NWO	AAA	22	155	19	4	4	3	14	15	45	4	0	.204/.281/.358
2019	MIA	MLB	23	35	3	1	0	1	3	4	11	0	0	.161/.257/.290

Breakout: 7% Improve: 14% Collapse: 2% Attrition: 7% MLB: 17%
Comparables: Carlos Asuaje, Brandon Lowe, Travis Denker

Slowly but surely, Diaz is turning into someone who looks like a future starting second baseman. A shortstop while in Milwaukee, his poor range forced him to move to the keystone, where his bat should still play. And really, that's his main draw. Diaz features plus power, the kind that can scrape out 25 home runs in the majors in his better years. He's earning himself a reputation as a Three True Outcomes player thanks to excellent walk rates in the minors to go with strikeout rates that hover around 25 percent. There's still room to grow in the contact department, where he needs to stop expanding the zone and use his quick bat speed. There's a strong chance he debuts later this year.

YEAR	TEAM	LVL	AGE	PA	DRC+	VORP	BABIP	BRR	FRAA	WARP
2016	WIS	A	20	587	141	37.7	.332	2.5	SS(90): -0.1, 2B(41): 1.0	4.3
2017	CAR	A+	21	455	105	14.8	.283	0.1	2B(70): -1.9, SS(32): -4.8	0.0
2018	JAX	AA	22	356	122	22.5	.325	0.0	2B(82): 2.1	1.4
2018	NWO	AAA	22	155	65	-2.0	.278	0.8	2B(35): -1.6	-0.4
2019	MIA	MLB	23	35	68	-0.1	.262	0.0	2B 0	0.0

Miami Marlins 2019

Joe Dunand SS

Born: 09/20/95   Age: 23   Bats: R   Throws: R
Height: 6'2"   Weight: 205   Origin: Round 2, 2017 Draft (#51 overall)

YEAR	TEAM	LVL	AGE	PA	R	2B	3B	HR	RBI	BB	K	SB	CS	AVG/OBP/SLG
2018	JUP	A+	22	273	39	8	1	7	42	20	54	2	0	.263/.326/.391
2018	JAX	AA	22	239	25	13	0	7	28	16	71	0	1	.212/.276/.369
2019	MIA	MLB	23	251	21	10	0	8	28	11	78	0	0	.189/.230/.333

Breakout: 34%   Improve: 42%   Collapse: 1%   Attrition: 28%   MLB: 42%
Comparables: Tim Beckham, Orlando Calixte, Derek Dietrich

It was a tale of two seasons for Dunand. He walked with his chin up and a little pep in his step for 66 games at High-A, where he didn't outperform the league but certainly didn't flounder. A promotion to Double-A produced a record scratch and stopped him in his tracks. While he maintained his average power, his strikeouts soared and he cratered everywhere else. The Fish are insistent on keeping him at shortstop, which will help his bat play. But he has a lot of adjustments to make in order to keep moving on up. Oh, and something something nephew of Alex Rodriguez.

YEAR	TEAM	LVL	AGE	PA	DRC+	VORP	BABIP	BRR	FRAA	WARP
2018	JUP	A+	22	273	116	14.8	.305	1.1	SS(62): 0.2	1.2
2018	JAX	AA	22	239	77	9.4	.277	-0.8	SS(60): -0.6	-0.2
2019	MIA	MLB	23	251	46	-7.0	.243	-0.5	SS 0	-0.8

Monte Harrison CF

Born: 08/10/95 Age: 23 Bats: R Throws: R
Height: 6'3" Weight: 220 Origin: Round 2, 2014 Draft (#50 overall)

YEAR	TEAM	LVL	AGE	PA	R	2B	3B	HR	RBI	BB	K	SB	CS	AVG/OBP/SLG
2016	WIS	A	20	298	34	11	1	6	37	20	97	8	3	.221/.294/.337
2017	WIS	A	21	261	32	12	1	11	32	29	70	11	3	.265/.359/.475
2017	CAR	A+	21	252	41	16	1	10	35	14	69	16	1	.278/.341/.487
2018	JAX	AA	22	583	85	20	3	19	48	44	215	28	9	.240/.316/.399
2019	MIA	MLB	23	35	4	1	0	1	4	1	13	1	0	*.182/.229/.303*

Breakout: 9% Improve: 19% Collapse: 4% Attrition: 15% MLB: 29%
Comparables: Trayce Thompson, Joe Benson, Franchy Cordero

It's drool-worthy to think of what Harrison could accomplish on a baseball field if his plate discipline is anything other than horrific. At 6-foot-3 and 220 pounds, he's a chiseled specimen, built like an NFL linebacker with plus power and speed as well a cannon for an arm. But in his first stint at Double-A he struggled mightily, with his 215 strikeouts pacing all of the minors. He has a bad habit of selling out for power and gets eaten alive by off-speed pitches as he still learns to time his massive leg kick. But he stayed healthy all season, which was a serious concern in the past. Harrison is the type of prospect to whom you give significant leash because the ceiling is an All-Star if it clicks.

YEAR	TEAM	LVL	AGE	PA	DRC+	VORP	BABIP	BRR	FRAA	WARP
2016	WIS	A	20	298	78	0.4	.321	1.0	CF(48): -0.7, RF(14): 1.0	-0.2
2017	WIS	A	21	261	132	21.9	.333	1.3	CF(62): 1.6	1.7
2017	CAR	A+	21	252	126	21.4	.358	3.3	CF(32): -1.8, RF(24): 2.1	1.3
2018	JAX	AA	22	583	96	28.5	.368	3.6	CF(121): -8.0, RF(14): 0.4	0.1
2019	MIA	MLB	23	35	41	-1.3	.260	0.1	LF 0	-0.1

Osiris Johnson SS

Born: 10/18/00   Age: 18   Bats: R   Throws: R
Height: 6'0"   Weight: 181   Origin: Round 2, 2018 Draft (#53 overall)

YEAR	TEAM	LVL	AGE	PA	R	2B	3B	HR	RBI	BB	K	SB	CS	AVG/OBP/SLG
2018	MRL	RK	17	111	12	8	2	1	13	4	19	7	2	.301/.333/.447
2018	GRB	A	17	88	4	3	0	2	6	1	34	0	2	.188/.205/.294
2019	MIA	MLB	18	251	15	6	0	5	21	1	99	1	1	.136/.137/.228

Comparables: Adalberto Mondesi, Wilmer Flores, Tommy Brown

The 53rd overall pick in the 2018 draft impressed so much in his professional debut that the Marlins jumped him from rookie ball to Low-A as a 17-year-old. It was an aggressive (and likely unnecessary) promotion, but shows how much the organization likes Johnson. He won't be as good as cousin Jimmy Rollins, but Johnson does project to stay on the dirt after he improved his defense enough to avoid getting relegated to the outfield. Often described as twitchy, he has a habit of pulling the ball, which might hinder him down the line against more advanced pitching. The athleticism is there, as is the frame for perhaps a touch more power.

YEAR	TEAM	LVL	AGE	PA	DRC+	VORP	BABIP	BRR	FRAA	WARP
2018	MRL	RK	17	111	114	8.7	.353	1.1	SS(23): 1.5	0.5
2018	GRB	A	17	88	29	-5.1	.280	-1.3	SS(23): -6.3	-1.2
2019	MIA	MLB	18	251	-15	-25.7	.193	0.4	SS -3	-3.1

Victor Victor Mesa CF
Born: 07/20/96   Age: 22   Bats: R   Throws: R
Height: 6'0"   Weight: 185   Origin: International Free Agent, 2018

Being the top international prospect in a class brings with it lofty expectations. Signed by the Marlins for $5.25 million, the man with two first names raised those expectations even higher by holding out for weeks until the Marlins built up enough pool money to ensure he and his younger brother would have a home in the Cuban-centric Miami culture. Mesa, the son of legendary Cuban star Victor Mesa, joined the Serie Nacional, Cuba's top professional league, as a 16-year-old under the tutelage of his father. He struggled initially, but in his second year he acclimated and won the Gold Glove. It kick-started a strong career that saw him climb to the ranks of a young superstar. As a whole, the dynamic center fielder is a force on both sides of the ball. He's a plus defender with enough speed and arm to patrol center for the Marlins for years to come. At the plate, there are the makings of a future plus hit tool with enough pull-side power to get into double-digit home runs. He has the speed to notch 30 or more bases in a season. Though he'll be 22 when the season begins, expect him to get a full year of seasoning in the minors, likely jumping three or maybe four levels as he shakes off the rust of someone who hasn't played in over a year. The Fish won't debut him until 2020 at the earliest. He's no organizational savior, but he represents a major change for how the team operates going forward.

Brian Miller OF

Born: 08/20/95 Age: 23 Bats: L Throws: R
Height: 6'1" Weight: 186 Origin: Round 1, 2017 Draft (#36 overall)

YEAR	TEAM	LVL	AGE	PA	R	2B	3B	HR	RBI	BB	K	SB	CS	AVG/OBP/SLG
2017	GRB	A	21	258	42	17	1	1	28	23	35	21	6	.322/.384/.416
2018	JUP	A+	22	276	28	13	3	0	29	14	27	19	6	.324/.358/.398
2018	JAX	AA	22	287	29	8	2	0	14	18	39	21	7	.267/.319/.313
2019	MIA	MLB	23	251	29	8	1	4	19	8	45	11	3	.240/.264/.334

Breakout: 6% Improve: 10% Collapse: 0% Attrition: 7% MLB: 11%
Comparables: Ben Gamel, Alex Romero, Whit Merrifield

Fresh off a 40-steal season split between High-A and Double-A, Miller showcased the type of player he could be in the majors. Though not an 80-grade burner, he maximizes his plus speed on the bases and in the outfield, where experience should allow him to overcome a fringy arm in center field. Miller has a knack for making contact, which leads to minimal strikeout rates, but his linear swing portends to 30-grade power in the future. If all breaks right, the former 36th overall pick in the 2016 draft can be an everyday player, but the influx of outfield prospects in the organization ensures he'll have to earn such a spot.

YEAR	TEAM	LVL	AGE	PA	DRC+	VORP	BABIP	BRR	FRAA	WARP
2017	GRB	A	21	258	146	15.7	.374	0.9	CF(35): 1.9, RF(13): -0.4	1.9
2018	JUP	A+	22	276	124	17.0	.358	0.7	CF(33): -1.5, LF(19): 0.2	0.8
2018	JAX	AA	22	287	88	4.1	.314	0.8	LF(49): 0.1, RF(12): 0.0	-0.3
2019	MIA	MLB	23	251	57	-3.9	.275	1.0	LF 1, CF 0	-0.2

Tristan Pompey OF

Born: 03/23/97 Age: 22 Bats: B Throws: R
Height: 6'4" Weight: 200 Origin: Round 3, 2018 Draft (#89 overall)

YEAR	TEAM	LVL	AGE	PA	R	2B	3B	HR	RBI	BB	K	SB	CS	AVG/OBP/SLG
2018	GRB	A	21	103	12	4	0	2	9	16	22	5	3	.314/.422/.430
2018	JUP	A+	21	101	13	5	0	1	13	13	21	4	1	.291/.396/.384
2019	MIA	MLB	22	251	24	7	0	6	24	20	72	4	2	.201/.266/.308

Breakout: 6% Improve: 18% Collapse: 0% Attrition: 11% MLB: 20%
Comparables: Aaron Hicks, Ryan Kalish, Daniel Fields

Brother of Blue Jays prospect Dalton Pompey, Tristan carries a more tantalizing all-around profile. The outfielder has played all three positions, but defensive limitations could point to a career in left field. The bat is good enough to play there, though. He's a switch-hitter who shows above-average raw power from both sides, exhibits a great eye at the plate and has enough speed to consistently reach double-digit steals early in his career. A 20-20 profile is not out of the question for the 2018 third-round pick.

YEAR	TEAM	LVL	AGE	PA	DRC+	VORP	BABIP	BRR	FRAA	WARP
2018	GRB	A	21	103	142	6.5	.403	-0.8	LF(10): -1.4, CF(5): -1.0	0.1
2018	JUP	A+	21	101	121	6.6	.375	1.1	CF(16): -3.8	0.0
2019	MIA	MLB	22	251	57	-4.9	.262	-0.2	CF -3, LF -1	-0.9

Harold Ramirez   RF

Born: 09/06/94   Age: 24   Bats: R   Throws: R
Height: 5'10"   Weight: 220   Origin: International Free Agent, 2011

YEAR	TEAM	LVL	AGE	PA	R	2B	3B	HR	RBI	BB	K	SB	CS	AVG/OBP/SLG
2016	ALT	AA	21	414	58	16	7	2	49	21	66	7	10	.306/.354/.401
2017	NHP	AA	22	490	46	19	2	6	53	32	65	5	3	.266/.320/.358
2018	NHP	AA	23	505	60	37	0	11	70	27	88	16	2	.320/.365/.471
2019	MIA	MLB	24	251	24	10	1	6	27	8	52	3	1	.248/.280/.372

Breakout: 6%   Improve: 18%   Collapse: 0%   Attrition: 16%   MLB: 22%
Comparables: Jamie Hoffmann, Ben Francisco, Mikie Mahtook

While there's no one tried-and-true path to major-league success, you'll rarely be steered wrong by a .300 batting average and double-digit stolen bases. Just ask Ramirez, who contested his indefinite exile in Double-A with a long-awaited breakout at the plate, and an MVP nod during the Fisher Cats' Eastern League championship run, to boot. Formerly a top prospect with the Pirates and allowed to walk as a minor-league free agent after last season by the Blue Jays, he hooked on with the Marlins and could fight his way onto the big-league roster at some point.

YEAR	TEAM	LVL	AGE	PA	DRC+	VORP	BABIP	BRR	FRAA	WARP
2016	ALT	AA	21	414	106	17.2	.363	2.4	CF(67): -8.0, RF(14): -1.7	0.1
2017	NHP	AA	22	490	84	-0.5	.296	-2.3	RF(73): 0.3, LF(25): -3.4	-1.5
2018	NHP	AA	23	505	131	31.3	.371	2.5	RF(61): -2.7, LF(18): -0.5	1.7
2019	MIA	MLB	24	251	74	-1.3	.292	-0.2	RF -1, LF 0	-0.3

JT Riddle SS

Born: 10/12/91　Age: 27　Bats: L　Throws: R
Height: 6'1"　Weight: 180　Origin: Round 13, 2013 Draft (#382 overall)

YEAR	TEAM	LVL	AGE	PA	R	2B	3B	HR	RBI	BB	K	SB	CS	AVG/OBP/SLG
2016	JAX	AA	24	429	49	18	4	3	51	33	72	5	1	.278/.332/.368
2016	NWO	AAA	24	57	4	2	0	1	2	1	9	1	0	.268/.281/.357
2017	NWO	AAA	25	64	9	4	1	2	6	1	8	1	0	.286/.297/.476
2017	MIA	MLB	25	247	20	13	1	3	31	12	50	0	2	.250/.282/.355
2018	NWO	AAA	26	91	17	4	1	3	19	8	15	2	0	.346/.400/.531
2018	MIA	MLB	26	332	28	10	4	9	36	20	67	0	3	.231/.277/.377
2019	MIA	MLB	27	398	38	15	3	10	43	24	81	2	1	.243/.293/.383

Breakout: 12%　Improve: 49%　Collapse: 15%　Attrition: 23%　MLB: 90%
Comparables: Zack Cozart, Eduardo Escobar, Josh Wilson

Riddle stood at the plate in his final game of the season. His gaze wandered to the oversized scoreboard in Marlins Park, probably built to be that large to distract from the empty blue seats, he thought. His slash line, ranking as one of the worst in baseball for shortstops with at least 300 plate appearances, shone bright on the board. As the smattering of fans grew impatient with how long he was taking to begin his at-bat, he reached for his neck and began peeling away the silicone. It was a mask. The fans gasped once the man's identity had been revealed. All this time they had assumed this new player was traded from the organization more than a year ago. Adeiny Hechavarria breathed deeply and exhaled with a devilish smile. The madman had never left.

YEAR	TEAM	LVL	AGE	PA	DRC+	VORP	BABIP	BRR	FRAA	WARP
2016	JAX	AA	24	429	103	20.0	.331	1.0	SS(71): 1.0, 2B(21): -0.2	1.1
2016	NWO	AAA	24	57	85	1.0	.304	-0.8	SS(13): -1.8, 2B(1): 0.0	-0.2
2017	NWO	AAA	25	64	96	4.3	.302	-0.3	SS(16): 0.9	0.3
2017	MIA	MLB	25	247	68	4.1	.300	0.7	SS(69): 1.5	0.4
2018	NWO	AAA	26	91	135	14.1	.391	1.3	SS(21): 2.0	1.0
2018	MIA	MLB	26	332	83	10.1	.266	1.7	SS(95): 8.1	1.8
2019	MIA	MLB	27	398	79	8.0	.280	-0.5	SS 2	0.7

Miami Marlins 2019

Connor Scott CF
Born: 10/08/99   Age: 19   Bats: L   Throws: L
Height: 6'4"   Weight: 180   Origin: Round 1, 2018 Draft (#13 overall)

YEAR	TEAM	LVL	AGE	PA	R	2B	3B	HR	RBI	BB	K	SB	CS	AVG/OBP/SLG
2018	MRL	RK	18	119	15	1	4	0	8	14	29	8	5	.223/.319/.311
2018	GRB	A	18	89	4	2	0	1	5	10	27	1	3	.211/.295/.276
2019	MIA	MLB	19	251	20	1	0	5	16	11	93	2	2	.121/.159/.193

Breakout: 6%   Improve: 8%   Collapse: 0%   Attrition: 3%   MLB: 10%
Comparables: Carlos Tocci, Engel Beltre, Nomar Mazara

The 13th overall pick in 2018 and the first under the new Marlins regime, Scott has raw potential but a long way to go to achieve it. The center fielder's frame is very projectable, with the possibility of adding two grades of power with more muscle, an enticing thought for someone with plus speed. For now, he has strong plate discipline and contact problems, especially with off-speed stuff. However, considering his age (and an unusually aggressive promotion to the Sally), it's hard to criticize for now. Don't get stars in your eyes with the unfair Kyle Tucker comparisons, but the foundation is there for Scott to turn into a good defensive outfielder with enough bat to make him a future regular.

YEAR	TEAM	LVL	AGE	PA	DRC+	VORP	BABIP	BRR	FRAA	WARP
2018	MRL	RK	18	119	89	0.5	.307	-1.2	CF(22): -1.6	-0.4
2018	GRB	A	18	89	58	-2.5	.300	-1.9	CF(22): -3.0	-0.8
2019	MIA	MLB	19	251	-13	-24.7	.166	0.0	CF -3	-2.9

Edward Cabrera   RHP

Born: 04/13/98   Age: 21   Bats: R   Throws: R
Height: 6'4"   Weight: 175   Origin: International Free Agent, 2015

YEAR	TEAM	LVL	AGE	W	L	SV	G	GS	IP	H	HR	BB/9	K/9	K	GB%	BABIP
2016	MRL	RK	18	2	6	0	11	7	47	54	1	1.9	5.4	28	41%	.331
2017	BAT	A-	19	1	3	0	13	6	35^2	42	1	2.0	8.1	32	55%	.350
2018	GRB	A	20	4	8	0	22	22	100^1	105	11	3.8	8.3	93	44%	.329
2019	*MIA*	*MLB*	*21*	*4*	*6*	*0*	*28*	*14*	*77^1*	*81*	*12*	*4.0*	*6.8*	*58*	*40%*	*.306*

Breakout: 0%   Improve: 0%   Collapse: 0%   Attrition: 1%   MLB: 1%
Comparables: Jamie Callahan, James Houser, Tyler Clippard

Believe it or not, there is such a thing as a pop-up prospect in an organization like the Marlins, and with his size and arsenal Cabrera certainly qualifies. He projects to fill out and add durability and a touch more velocity. It's not like he needs more ticks on his fastball, though. He already added 2-3 mph last year and sits in the mid-90s, maxing out at 97. He complements his heater with a slider that flashes above average. Cabrera performed well nearly two years younger than the average competition in 2018, but he has a ways to go as the overall package is still raw. His changeup is almost nonexistent and inconsistencies in his make-you-lose-your-hat windup are holding back his command.

YEAR	TEAM	LVL	AGE	WHIP	ERA	DRA	WARP	MPH	FB%	WHF	CSP
2016	MRL	RK	18	1.36	4.21	2.80	1.5				
2017	BAT	A-	19	1.40	5.30	4.64	0.2				
2018	GRB	A	20	1.47	4.22	6.61	-1.7				
2019	*MIA*	*MLB*	*21*	*1.49*	*5.20*	*6.14*	*-1.0*				

Robert Dugger RHP

Born: 07/03/95 Age: 23 Bats: R Throws: R
Height: 6'2" Weight: 180 Origin: Round 18, 2016 Draft (#537 overall)

YEAR	TEAM	LVL	AGE	W	L	SV	G	GS	IP	H	HR	BB/9	K/9	K	GB%	BABIP
2016	MRN	RK	20	0	0	2	4	0	8^2	6	0	1.0	9.3	9	61%	.261
2016	EVE	A-	20	2	1	0	6	6	26^1	25	5	3.4	8.5	25	75%	.282
2017	CLN	A	21	4	1	2	22	9	72	55	4	2.0	8.6	69	51%	.263
2017	MOD	A+	21	2	5	0	9	9	45^2	49	4	3.2	9.3	47	40%	.341
2018	JUP	A+	22	3	1	0	7	7	41^1	40	2	1.5	7.4	34	57%	.306
2018	JAX	AA	22	7	6	0	18	18	109^1	100	13	3.0	8.8	107	36%	.296
2019	MIA	MLB	23	6	8	1	34	19	120^2	113	18	3.5	8.2	110	44%	.294

Breakout: 5%   Improve: 8%   Collapse: 11%   Attrition: 18%   MLB: 23%
Comparables: Chih-Wei Hu, Daniel Mengden, P.J. Conlon

Part of the three-man return from Seattle for Dee Gordon, Dugger is shaping up to be a win for the Mariners' scouting department, except the Marlins are set to reap the benefits. A former 18th-round pick in 2016, on the mound he looks like he's pitching at 1.5X speed thanks to his extremely quick tempo and cross-body delivery. His fastball is his best pitch and clocks in at 92-93 mph with movement, but he lacks command of it. His slider is easily his second-best pitch, an above-average offering that he uses to put away lefties. It's now a question of whether Dugger's changeup or curveball can develop far enough so that he can stick in a rotation and become a fourth or fifth starter, or if he falters and is sent packing to the bullpen.

YEAR	TEAM	LVL	AGE	WHIP	ERA	DRA	WARP	MPH	FB%	WHF	CSP
2016	MRN	RK	20	0.81	1.04	2.79	0.2				
2016	EVE	A-	20	1.33	5.47	3.86	0.4				
2017	CLN	A	21	0.99	2.00	3.29	1.6				
2017	MOD	A+	21	1.42	3.94	4.06	0.6				
2018	JUP	A+	22	1.14	2.40	3.71	0.8				
2018	JAX	AA	22	1.24	3.79	5.46	-0.1				
2019	MIA	MLB	23	1.33	4.61	5.44	-0.3				

Tommy Eveld RHP

Born: 12/30/93 Age: 25 Bats: R Throws: R
Height: 6'5" Weight: 195 Origin: Round 9, 2016 Draft (#269 overall)

YEAR	TEAM	LVL	AGE	W	L	SV	G	GS	IP	H	HR	BB/9	K/9	K	GB%	BABIP
2016	YAK	A-	22	2	1	2	24	0	29	17	0	2.5	9.6	31	51%	.243
2017	KNC	A	23	1	0	14	22	0	27^2	10	0	2.6	10.7	33	59%	.169
2017	VIS	A+	23	0	5	2	19	0	22	22	1	4.5	10.6	26	64%	.350
2018	VIS	A+	24	2	2	12	32	0	36^1	29	1	1.7	10.4	42	54%	.298
2018	JAX	AA	24	1	1	3	10	0	9^2	6	0	2.8	13.0	14	38%	.286
2019	MIA	MLB	25	2	1	2	39	0	41^2	35	5	3.8	9.4	44	46%	.291

Breakout: 3%   Improve: 7%   Collapse: 7%   Attrition: 13%   MLB: 15%
Comparables: Adam Kolarek, Rowan Wick, Edgar Santana

Originally a quarterback at the University of South Florida, Eveld never saw a snap after tearing his ACL. The 6-foot-5 athlete then tried to juggle being a wide receiver instead, while also making the baseball team. Though a second ACL tear set him back, he played enough baseball to show that he had the goods on the mound. He has a four-pitch mix but relies heavily on his 92-95 mph fastball and a slider that sometimes mirrors a cutter thanks to how hard he throws it. He's a little on the older side but has a realistic chance at a setup role, perhaps by the end of 2019.

YEAR	TEAM	LVL	AGE	WHIP	ERA	DRA	WARP	MPH	FB%	WHF	CSP
2016	YAK	A-	22	0.86	1.86	3.64	0.4				
2017	KNC	A	23	0.65	0.33	3.59	0.4				
2017	VIS	A+	23	1.50	5.73	3.26	0.4				
2018	VIS	A+	24	0.99	1.24	2.48	1.0				
2018	JAX	AA	24	0.93	0.93	2.93	0.2				
2019	MIA	MLB	25	1.26	3.86	4.58	0.2				

Miami Marlins 2019

Riley Ferrell   RHP
Born: 10/18/93   Age: 25   Bats: R   Throws: R
Height: 6'2"   Weight: 200   Origin: Round 3, 2015 Draft (#79 overall)

YEAR	TEAM	LVL	AGE	W	L	SV	G	GS	IP	H	HR	BB/9	K/9	K	GB%	BABIP
2016	LNC	A+	22	0	1	4	8	0	10	9	1	1.8	12.6	14	62%	.348
2017	CCH	AA	23	2	2	4	36	0	52	51	2	2.4	9.5	55	52%	.348
2018	CCH	AA	24	2	2	7	21	0	23^2	14	1	6.8	12.5	33	47%	.260
2018	FRE	AAA	24	2	1	2	22	0	28	34	4	5.1	10.9	34	38%	.390
2019	MIA	MLB	25	1	1	0	22	0	22	20	2	4.5	9.9	25	45%	.297

Breakout: 14%   Improve: 18%   Collapse: 12%   Attrition: 25%   MLB: 33%
Comparables: Jimmie Sherfy, Joe Paterson, Jaye Chapman

Ferrell combines a plus fastball, a plus slider and a consistently high strikeout rate dating back to his college days. The next time you wonder why there are so many strikeouts in baseball, remember that this profile is now common enough that Ferrell was exposed to the Rule 5 draft, where the Marlins snagged the potential late-inning reliever from the Astros. He'll have to remain on the active roster all season to stick in Miami, but if any team has reason to show patience with a talented young pitcher no matter the growing pains, it's certainly the Marlins.

YEAR	TEAM	LVL	AGE	WHIP	ERA	DRA	WARP	MPH	FB%	WHF	CSP
2016	LNC	A+	22	1.10	1.80	3.43	0.2				
2017	CCH	AA	23	1.25	3.81	3.24	1.0				
2018	CCH	AA	24	1.35	1.90	3.00	0.5				
2018	FRE	AAA	24	1.79	6.75	3.80	0.4				
2019	MIA	MLB	25	1.38	4.04	4.47	0.1				

Zac Gallen RHP

Born: 08/03/95   Age: 23   Bats: R   Throws: R
Height: 6'2"   Weight: 191   Origin: Round 3, 2016 Draft (#106 overall)

YEAR	TEAM	LVL	AGE	W	L	SV	G	GS	IP	H	HR	BB/9	K/9	K	GB%	BABIP
2016	CRD	RK	20	0	0	1	6	3	9^2	7	0	0.0	14.0	15	48%	.333
2017	PMB	A+	21	5	2	0	9	9	55^2	44	1	1.6	9.1	56	48%	.283
2017	SFD	AA	21	4	5	0	13	13	71^1	76	8	2.4	5.3	42	42%	.292
2017	MEM	AAA	21	1	1	0	4	4	20^2	18	2	2.6	10.0	23	47%	.314
2018	NWO	AAA	22	8	9	0	25	25	133^1	148	14	3.2	9.2	136	41%	.351
2019	MIA	MLB	23	6	8	0	22	22	118^2	110	16	3.2	8.8	116	42%	.302

Breakout: 11%   Improve: 15%   Collapse: 9%   Attrition: 21%   MLB: 27%
Comparables: Taylor Guerrieri, Alex Cobb, Brady Rodgers

Despite being arguably only the third-best of four prospects acquired from St. Louis as the Marlins' return in the Marcell Ozuna trade, Gallen has the type of profile that could reasonably ensure he ends up producing the most value of the group. Gallen checks every box in the Not A Flamethrower But Has Command Starter Pack: A four-pitch mix (fastball, cutter, curveball, changeup) that doesn't feature any plus pitch, a chance at above-average command at peak, sequencing knowledge and a slightly undersized build. After an encouraging season at Triple-A, Gallen should see a fair amount of time in the major-league rotation this year at age 23.

YEAR	TEAM	LVL	AGE	WHIP	ERA	DRA	WARP	MPH	FB%	WHF	CSP
2016	CRD	RK	20	0.72	1.86	1.29	0.5				
2017	PMB	A+	21	0.97	1.62	3.39	1.2				
2017	SFD	AA	21	1.33	3.79	4.08	0.9				
2017	MEM	AAA	21	1.16	3.48	4.02	0.4				
2018	NWO	AAA	22	1.47	3.64	3.95	2.4				
2019	MIA	MLB	23	1.27	4.12	4.88	0.6				

Miami Marlins 2019

Braxton Garrett   LHP
Born: 08/05/97   Age: 21   Bats: L   Throws: L
Height: 6'3"   Weight: 190   Origin: Round 1, 2016 Draft (#7 overall)

YEAR	TEAM	LVL	AGE	W	L	SV	G	GS	IP	H	HR	BB/9	K/9	K	GB%	BABIP
2017	GRB	A	19	1	0	0	4	4	15¹	13	3	3.5	9.4	16	49%	.250
2019	MIA	MLB	21	2	3	0	8	8	35¹	34	5	4.2	8.0	31	42%	.300

Breakout: 1%   Improve: 2%   Collapse: 1%   Attrition: 3%   MLB: 5%
Comparables: Tyrell Jenkins, Elvis Araujo, Keury Mella

It's been more than two years since the Marlins drafted Garrett seventh overall out of an Alabama high school and we barely know more about him now than we did back then. The southpaw underwent Tommy John surgery in July of 2017, setting him up for a second-half return this upcoming season. But in the 15 1/3 innings he pitched before going down, he showed glimpses of why the Marlins liked him so much as a prep arm. His curveball is a future plus pitch that hovers between 76-80 mph, the kind he can spot and play well off his average fastball. His changeup is a potential above-average offering, too. Because he was drafted out of high school time is still on his side, but he can ill afford any more loss of development.

YEAR	TEAM	LVL	AGE	WHIP	ERA	DRA	WARP	MPH	FB%	WHF	CSP
2017	GRB	A	19	1.24	2.93	2.87	0.4				
2019	MIA	MLB	21	1.42	4.75	5.61	-0.1				

Jorge Guzman RHP

Born: 01/28/96 Age: 23 Bats: R Throws: R
Height: 6'2" Weight: 182 Origin: International Free Agent, 2014

YEAR	TEAM	LVL	AGE	W	L	SV	G	GS	IP	H	HR	BB/9	K/9	K	GB%	BABIP
2016	AST	RK	20	1	1	0	7	4	17^1	4	0	5.2	13.0	25	77%	.129
2016	GRV	RK	20	2	3	0	6	4	22^2	25	1	2.8	11.5	29	56%	.387
2017	STA	A-	21	5	3	0	13	13	66^2	51	4	2.4	11.9	88	55%	.311
2018	JUP	A+	22	0	9	0	21	21	96	84	7	6.0	9.5	101	40%	.303
2019	MIA	MLB	23	4	7	0	18	18	78^1	72	12	5.8	9.1	79	44%	.301

Breakout: 2% Improve: 2% Collapse: 2% Attrition: 2% MLB: 4%
Comparables: Steve Johnson, J.A. Happ, Josh Outman

Not even Guzman's 99 mph fastball can distract you from realizing how much of a step back he took in 2018. The prized prospect acquired from the Yankees in the Giancarlo Stanton trade turned in a 15 percent walk rate in 96 innings, good for third-worst in the minors had he qualified. His strikeouts also regressed in his High-A debut; after easily crossing the 30 percent whiff mark in his past seasons, he finished at 23 percent. It was a rude awakening for Guzman, who tilted the scale a little closer to "future reliever" after showing he couldn't support his 80-grade fastball with a below-average changeup and average-at-best curveball. His control and command are still missing, and at 22 years old he can't fall back on age as an excuse.

YEAR	TEAM	LVL	AGE	WHIP	ERA	DRA	WARP	MPH	FB%	WHF	CSP
2016	AST	RK	20	0.81	3.12	3.03	0.5				
2016	GRV	RK	20	1.41	4.76	2.29	0.8				
2017	STA	A-	21	1.03	2.30	2.14	2.4				
2018	JUP	A+	22	1.54	4.03	4.95	0.4				
2019	MIA	MLB	23	1.56	5.14	6.05	-0.7				

Miami Marlins 2019

Tyler Kolek   RHP
Born: 12/15/95   Age: 23   Bats: R   Throws: R
Height: 6'5"   Weight: 260   Origin: Round 1, 2014 Draft (#2 overall)

YEAR	TEAM	LVL	AGE	W	L	SV	G	GS	IP	H	HR	BB/9	K/9	K	GB%	BABIP
2018	BAT	A-	22	1	2	0	8	0	14	12	0	4.5	7.7	12	44%	.279
2019	MIA	MLB	23	0	4	0	9	6	27^2	30	6	13.2	6.5	20	43%	.303

Breakout: 1%   Improve: 2%   Collapse: 0%   Attrition: 2%   MLB: 2%
Comparables: Pedro Villarreal, Kevin McGowan, Mike Parisi

Have you ever decided to watch a movie only because it featured your favorite director or actor? Maybe you trusted the last piece of work they turned in and decided "screw it, I won't even care what this movie is about because it has their fingerprints!" This is what the Marlins did in the 2014 draft. The feature presentation *Tyler Kolek* was playing, directed by Josh Beckett and produced by "Large Texan Righty" studios. The movie bombed. After costing $6 million to produce, there's a chance Kolek will never be seen by a single member of the audience for which it was intended.

YEAR	TEAM	LVL	AGE	WHIP	ERA	DRA	WARP	MPH	FB%	WHF	CSP
2018	BAT	A-	22	1.36	4.50	4.11	0.1				
2019	MIA	MLB	23	2.56	9.16	10.81	-1.8				

Nick Neidert RHP

Born: 11/20/96 Age: 22 Bats: R Throws: R
Height: 6'1" Weight: 180 Origin: Round 2, 2015 Draft (#60 overall)

YEAR	TEAM	LVL	AGE	W	L	SV	G	GS	IP	H	HR	BB/9	K/9	K	GB%	BABIP
2016	CLN	A	19	7	3	0	19	19	91	75	7	1.3	6.8	69	41%	.262
2017	MOD	A+	20	10	3	0	19	19	104^1	95	7	1.5	9.4	109	43%	.318
2017	ARK	AA	20	1	3	0	6	6	23^1	33	4	1.9	5.0	13	47%	.341
2018	JAX	AA	21	12	7	0	26	26	152^2	142	17	1.8	9.1	154	47%	.309
2019	MIA	MLB	22	0	1	0	2	2	10	9	1	2.2	7.8	9	41%	.294

Breakout: 16% Improve: 29% Collapse: 13% Attrition: 27% MLB: 54%
Comparables: Alex White, Erasmo Ramirez, Aaron Poreda

Neidert has old-man skills — the good kind that should lead him to a long and fruitful career in the majors. Living off advanced control and command, he takes his below-average fastball and masterfully sequences it with his nearly plus changeup and average curveball. It's how he's amassed a sub-2.0 BB/9 in his minor-league career. He peppers the fringes of the strike zone and induces weak contact. Neidert isn't just a pitch-to-contact guy, either, striking out more than a batter an inning last year. Don't be surprised if he takes on a significant role this upcoming season and ultimately becomes one of the more reliable no. 4 starters in baseball.

YEAR	TEAM	LVL	AGE	WHIP	ERA	DRA	WARP	MPH	FB%	WHF	CSP
2016	CLN	A	19	0.97	2.57	3.67	1.5				
2017	MOD	A+	20	1.07	2.76	3.16	2.6				
2017	ARK	AA	20	1.63	6.56	4.19	0.3				
2018	JAX	AA	21	1.13	3.24	3.79	2.8				
2019	MIA	MLB	22	1.17	3.76	4.25	0.1				

Trevor Rogers LHP

Born: 11/13/97 Age: 21 Bats: L Throws: L
Height: 6'6" Weight: 185 Origin: Round 1, 2017 Draft (#13 overall)

YEAR	TEAM	LVL	AGE	W	L	SV	G	GS	IP	H	HR	BB/9	K/9	K	GB%	BABIP
2018	GRB	A	20	2	7	0	17	17	72^2	86	4	3.3	10.5	85	48%	.394
2019	MIA	MLB	21	3	4	0	12	12	54^1	53	7	3.9	8.5	51	41%	.312

Comparables: Robbie Ross, John Gant, Christian Friedrich

Limbs. Limbs everywhere. Rogers' 6-foot-6 frame and three-quarters delivery from the left side display his long levers and allow him to get great extension as he delivers his pitches. His four-seamer sits 90-92 mph, but he can reach back for 95 when needed. His two-seamer is his ground-ball generator and his weapon against righties. His slider and changeup have nice velocity separation and project as future average offerings. As you might expect from someone so big on the mound, there are some command issues at present because of mechanics, but his low-effort delivery should aid in rectifying them. All in all it was a strong professional debut for Rogers in his first season after recovering from Tommy John surgery.

YEAR	TEAM	LVL	AGE	WHIP	ERA	DRA	WARP	MPH	FB%	WHF	CSP
2018	GRB	A	20	1.56	5.82	4.46	0.6				
2019	MIA	MLB	21	1.40	4.29	5.08	0.1				

Sixto Sanchez RHP

Born: 07/29/98 Age: 20 Bats: R Throws: R
Height: 6'0" Weight: 185 Origin: International Free Agent, 2015

YEAR	TEAM	LVL	AGE	W	L	SV	G	GS	IP	H	HR	BB/9	K/9	K	GB%	BABIP
2016	PHL	RK	17	5	0	0	11	11	54	33	0	1.3	7.3	44	57%	.236
2017	LWD	A	18	5	3	0	13	13	67^1	46	1	1.2	8.6	64	49%	.251
2017	CLR	A+	18	0	4	0	5	5	27^2	27	1	2.9	6.5	20	42%	.295
2018	CLR	A+	19	4	3	0	8	8	46^2	39	1	2.1	8.7	45	52%	.295
2019	MIA	MLB	20	3	3	0	9	9	46^2	42	5	3.0	8.0	42	47%	.294

Breakout: 4%   Improve: 8%   Collapse: 5%   Attrition: 14%   MLB: 17%
Comparables: Jacob Turner, Francis Martes, Ian Krol

It's prescriptivist to claim Sixto was destined to get hurt eventually, but reports of a teenager touching 102 with his fastball (while thrilling) are enough to plant a small seed of worry. Those worries grew and bore fruit in 2018, when Sanchez was forced to miss the majority of the season with elbow inflammation, assigned to the Arizona Fall League to make up for some of those lost outings, and then had to bail on that due to collarbone discomfort. It's no secret that Sixto's got impossibly powerful stuff for his or any age, but a healthy 2019 will go a long way toward assuaging doubts that his advanced arm will have shot its best bullets before he even gets to make his Phillies debut. Sanchez won't even turn 21 until the end of July, so any talk of his being "broken" or "damaged" on the heels of a lost half-season are far too premature. At the very least, we absolutely cannot be deprived of a second "Sixto" entry in the annals of baseball history. It's only just.

YEAR	TEAM	LVL	AGE	WHIP	ERA	DRA	WARP	MPH	FB%	WHF	CSP
2016	PHL	RK	17	0.76	0.50	2.61	1.9				
2017	LWD	A	18	0.82	2.41	2.93	1.9				
2017	CLR	A+	18	1.30	4.55	3.61	0.5				
2018	CLR	A+	19	1.07	2.51	3.67	0.9				
2019	MIA	MLB	20	1.25	4.05	4.80	0.3				

Miami Marlins 2019

Jordan Yamamoto RHP
Born: 05/11/96 Age: 23 Bats: R Throws: R
Height: 6'0" Weight: 185 Origin: Round 12, 2014 Draft (#356 overall)

YEAR	TEAM	LVL	AGE	W	L	SV	G	GS	IP	H	HR	BB/9	K/9	K	GB%	BABIP
2016	WIS	A	20	7	8	0	27	18	134¹	130	6	2.1	10.2	152	48%	.343
2017	CAR	A+	21	9	4	1	22	18	111	91	8	2.4	9.2	113	40%	.286
2018	JUP	A+	22	4	1	0	7	7	40²	26	0	1.8	10.4	47	44%	.268
2018	MRL	RK	22	1	0	0	3	3	11	5	1	1.6	12.3	15	64%	.190
2018	JAX	AA	22	1	0	0	3	3	17	12	1	2.1	12.2	23	45%	.282
2019	MIA	MLB	23	1	2	0	18	2	27	23	3	3.2	9.4	28	41%	.293

Breakout: 6% Improve: 9% Collapse: 15% Attrition: 20% MLB: 33%
Comparables: Austin Gomber, Jharel Cotton, Miguel Almonte

There's a non-zero chance that Yamamoto emerges as the best player acquired from the Brewers in the Christian Yelich trade, which included then-headliner Lewis Brinson, Monte Harrison and Isan Diaz. That's a loaded sentence to be sure, but also a testament to Yamamoto's arsenal and what he can do with it when healthy. He bookended the 2018 season with disabled list stints for his shoulder, but still carved some time in the Arizona Fall League. His above-average fastball and plus slider still play well with his short stride, and his strong control allows him to bust hitters in to rack up strikeouts. He's not a flashy guy, but the organization has to be thrilled with the returns on the former 12th rounder out of Hawaii.

YEAR	TEAM	LVL	AGE	WHIP	ERA	DRA	WARP	MPH	FB%	WHF	CSP
2016	WIS	A	20	1.20	3.82	2.99	3.2				
2017	CAR	A+	21	1.09	2.51	3.59	2.1				
2018	JUP	A+	22	0.84	1.55	2.89	1.2				
2018	MRL	RK	22	0.64	2.45	1.77	0.5				
2018	JAX	AA	22	0.94	2.12	4.05	0.3				
2019	MIA	MLB	23	1.21	3.46	3.99	0.3				

LINEOUTS

Hitters

HITTER	POS	TEAM	LVL	AGE	PA	R	2B	3B	HR	RBI	BB	K	SB	CS	AVG/OBP/SLG	DRC+	WARP
Pedro Alvarez	3B	BAL	MLB	31	127	18	2	0	8	18	16	36	0	0	.180/.283/.414	93	0.0
	3B	NOR	AAA	31	178	21	6	0	8	32	11	42	0	0	.285/.331/.467	132	0.6
Gabriel Guerrero	RF	PEN	AA	24	107	13	9	1	2	16	7	26	3	0	.296/.336/.469	100	0.6
	RF	LOU	AAA	24	432	64	15	4	17	65	23	97	1	3	.292/.326/.475	123	1.6
	RF	CIN	MLB	24	18	1	0	0	1	1	0	8	0	0	.167/.167/.333	71	0.0
Rosell Herrera	RF	CIN	MLB	25	13	0	0	0	0	0	0	5	0	1	.154/.154/.154	70	0.0
	RF	LOU	AAA	25	98	11	8	2	3	11	6	15	2	1	.267/.320/.500	124	0.2
	RF	OMA	AAA	25	41	8	3	2	1	5	5	7	4	1	.278/.366/.556	127	0.3
	RF	KCA	MLB	25	289	25	14	3	1	20	19	52	3	4	.238/.292/.325	71	-0.2
Bryan Holaday	C	MIA	MLB	30	166	7	5	0	1	16	10	29	0	0	.205/.261/.258	81	0.7
Dixon Machado	SS	DET	MLB	26	233	20	13	1	1	21	14	41	1	1	.206/.263/.290	70	0.1
	SS	TOL	AAA	26	171	19	5	0	1	8	18	28	4	2	.224/.321/.279	83	0.4
Deven Marrero	SS	ARI	MLB	27	85	11	1	1	0	7	6	23	3	0	.167/.224/.205	55	0.0
	SS	RNO	AAA	27	76	10	4	1	1	7	7	20	0	0	.227/.297/.364	60	-0.1
Peter O'Brien	RF	TUL	AA	27	112	12	3	0	7	22	10	44	0	0	.150/.241/.390	37	-1.1
	RF	JAX	AA	27	174	22	4	0	13	31	28	49	0	0	.215/.345/.514	135	0.2
	RF	NWO	AAA	27	135	22	6	0	10	33	20	40	1	0	.277/.385/.598	141	1.0
	RF	MIA	MLB	27	74	8	5	0	4	10	7	22	0	0	.273/.338/.530	102	0.3
Yadiel Rivera	3B	MIA	MLB	26	160	13	3	0	1	9	19	51	2	1	.173/.269/.216	55	0.0
Chad Wallach	C	NWO	AAA	26	174	20	7	0	3	16	20	47	0	1	.224/.324/.333	83	0.8
	C	MIA	MLB	26	52	4	1	0	1	5	4	23	0	0	.178/.275/.267	54	0.3

On a different but still terrible Orioles team, **Pedro Alvarez** might have had a role. Unfortunately the skill set of "hits for some power/poor defender" was filled many times over in 2018 by Baltimore's Stonehenge of Trumbo/Davis/Mancini. Not even an above-average walk rate could keep Alvarez safe from Norfolk, where an Achilles' tendon injury ended his season in late August. ⓥ **Gabriel Guerrero** is related to Vlad The Impaler, but he didn't get as lucky as his cousin, Vlad Jr., when it comes to the baseball genes. A bit of power returned last season, but the contact rate and strikeouts are too problematic for now. ⓥ A fringy, speed-based corner outfielder cut loose by the Reds (the Reds, for goodness sake!) in June, **Rosell Herrera** went on to accumulate over 300 plate appearances with the Royals, doing very poorly the two things he was supposed to do well: steal bases and take walks. ⓥ **Bryan Holaday**'s career OPS sank below .600 after a horrendous season at the plate, but he still provides defensive value thanks to being one of the better framing catchers in baseball. ⓥ If you're scavenging for Triple-A highlight reels, you're going to find **Dixon Machado** pick some crazy grounders. Because he can't hit worth a lick in the majors, the video quality is unlikely to be high-def. ⓥ Teams don't want to rely on a guy like **Deven Marrero**, but the Diamondbacks were forced to do so when early injuries pressed

Miami Marlins 2019

the journeyman into action. He provided solid defensive value, but he still can't hit. ⓧ Very little is known about the 17-year-old **Victor Mesa Jr.** He's a switch-hitter, he has a projectable body with below-average current offensive tools and his brother is rich now. ⓧ It's beginning to look like **Peter O'Brien** may not be the next great Yankees catcher. He could be the next Quad-A corner bat in Miami, though. ⓧ Of 392 batters that accrued at least 150 plate appearances last year, **Yadiel Rivera**'s .485 OPS was second-worst in baseball. Rarely does one number summarize a player, but in Rivera's case, that's about all you need to know. ⓧ **Chad Wallach** will continue to be known as Tim's son until he shows he's more than a third-string catcher who can't hit.

Pitchers

PITCHER	TEAM	LVL	AGE	W	L	SV	G	GS	IP	H	HR	BB/9	K/9	K	GB%	WHIP	ERA	DRA	WARP
Jeff Brigham	JAX	AA	26	4	1	0	7	7	38	27	1	2.1	9.7	41	41%	0.95	1.18	4.43	0.4
	NWO	AAA	26	5	2	0	9	9	52¹	53	7	2.2	8.3	48	30%	1.26	3.44	4.17	0.8
	MIA	MLB	26	0	4	0	4	4	16¹	16	2	7.2	6.6	12	20%	1.78	6.06	7.19	-0.4
Brett Graves	JAX	AA	25	1	1	0	5	1	12¹	13	2	4.4	7.3	10	58%	1.54	5.11	3.99	0.2
	MIA	MLB	25	1	1	1	21	0	33¹	41	3	3.2	5.7	21	47%	1.59	5.40	4.86	0.0
Elieser Hernandez	MIA	MLB	23	2	7	0	32	6	65²	68	11	3.7	6.2	45	30%	1.45	5.21	6.00	-0.7
Tyler Kinley	MIN	MLB	27	0	0	0	4	0	3¹	9	2	10.8	10.8	4	60%	3.90	24.30	2.63	0.1
	NWO	AAA	27	2	2	8	40	0	40	32	2	4.9	12.6	56	38%	1.35	2.92	2.42	1.2
	MIA	MLB	27	0	0	0	9	0	7²	6	0	4.7	10.6	9	55%	1.30	7.04	2.30	0.2
Pablo Lopez	JAX	AA	22	1	2	0	8	8	43²	30	3	1.6	10.5	51	42%	0.87	0.62	3.62	0.9
	NWO	AAA	22	1	1	0	4	4	18²	16	3	1.9	7.2	15	47%	1.07	3.38	3.93	0.3
	MIA	MLB	22	2	4	0	10	10	58²	56	8	2.8	7.1	46	50%	1.26	4.14	4.58	0.5
Ben Meyer	NWO	AAA	25	5	4	0	15	11	63²	67	4	2.7	6.9	49	43%	1.35	4.24	3.83	1.2
	MIA	MLB	25	0	0	0	13	0	19	26	2	6.6	4.3	9	44%	2.11	10.42	8.00	-0.7

Though **Jeff Brigham** has been a starter in the minors, he's limited by his over-reliance on a 91-94 mph fastball and a curveball, potentially pointing to a future as a reliever. ⓧ The Giants were so enamored with **Julian Fernandez**'s triple-digit velocity in the 2017 Rule 5 draft that they didn't care he was already 22 and hadn't graduated A-ball. Now he's 23, recovering from elbow surgery and off to the Marlins on a waiver claim. ⓧ **Brett Graves** was a starter in the Athletics' farm system two years ago. Now, still armed with a poor strikeout rate and uninspiring fastball, slider, and curveball combo, he's another faceless reliever in the back end of a bullpen. ⓧ A Rule 5 pick last year, **Elieser Hernandez** bucked all expectations and became a star in the bullpen. Nah, just kidding. He stunk. What else did you think would happen when an organization rushes you from High-A to the majors? ⓧ Marlins fan weeping over the loss of Kyle Barraclough need to look no further than **Tyler Kinley**, a righty with a power fastball and big slider and Barraclough's trademark exorbitant walk rates. ⓧ

With three average pitches and strong command, there's a path for **Pablo Lopez** to become a serviceable fifth starter. It's just a really boring one. ⚾ In 2017, **Ben Meyer** raised eyebrows with a sparkling strikeout-to-walk ratio, dominating the Sally and Florida State League. Given a new challenge in Triple-A and the majors last year, he flopped dramatically, losing the strikeouts and proving he couldn't cut it against left-handed batters. ⚾ **James Needy** earned a 40-man roster spot after being signed out of independent ball, but he missed all of 2018 with an injury and was promptly dropped from the roster. ⚾ **Chris O'Grady**'s 87 mph fastball from the left side makes it so he can't pitch to right-handed batters because they obliterate his offerings. If we're being honest, he shouldn't be pitching to lefties all that often either. ⚾ Overslot 2016 fourth-rounder **Chris Rodriguez** missed last season with a stress reaction in his lower back, and will likely see an innings limit heading into 2019. ⚾ When the season begins, **Drew Rucinski** will be a 30-year-old reliever with just 54 major-league innings under his belt, but several teams have been intrigued only to decide they didn't have the patience to give him a longer look.

Marlins Prospects

The State of the System:
When you trade for a lot of high-variance players to rebuild your farm system, well… you don't always get the good end of the variance.

The Top Ten:

1 Victor Victor Mesa   OF   OFP: 60   Likely: 50
ETA: Could be as soon as 2019. Or it could not be.
Born: 07/20/96   Age: 22   Bats: R   Throws: R   Height: 6'0"   Weight: 185
Origin: International Free Agent, 2018

The Report: I think everyone in baseball has made the Albert Almora comp by now, publicly and privately. We hate comps here at Baseball Prospectus, but this one makes sense. Like Almora, Victor Victor is a right-handed, defensively-minded center fielder who can hit, though not for much power. They're similarly built and they take a similar-looking swing.

It's not a perfect comparison, of course. We think Mesa will run more: He stole 40 bases in just 70 games in his last full season in Serie Nacional, and scuttlebutt had him putting up 60-yard-dash times in his private workout that would give him a couple grades of speed on Almora. And although there's broad agreement that Mesa will stick in center and can handle the bat, it remains to be seen whether he has Almora's keen overall baseball instincts. It's also probably worth noting when throwing this comp out that Almora would be playing more if the embarrassment of riches in the Cubs outfield didn't permit them to deploy him in a somewhat sheltered role. But if you're doing broad strokes, sure, it's an Albert Almora sort of profile.

The Risks: High. He hasn't played competitive baseball in a year. If he falls just a bit short of Almora's 2018 he might not be a regular. There's more disagreement on his power and speed projections than you'd like there to be. The quality of Serie Nacional has deteriorated enough that even the guys who have dominated there have needed to adjust to American pitching, and Mesa didn't always dominate there. There are all kinds of cultural and social challenges facing high-profile Cuban players coming over.

Bret Sayre's Fantasy Take: I'm a fan. Mesa is likely to make his strongest contributions in average and runs, as he should hit and hit at the top of the Marlins lineup in the not-to-distant future. He also has the speed to steal 30 bags if he so chooses, which only exacerbates the profile. If it all works, Mesa's upside probably looks pretty similar to 2018 Lorenzo Cain, who was a top-10 outfielder—which makes him a top-25 dynasty prospect and a strong candidate for the first pick in dynasty drafts this offseason.

2 Sandy Alcantara   RHP   OFP: 60   Likely: 50   ETA: Debuted in 2017
Born: 09/07/95   Age: 23   Bats: R   Throws: R   Height: 6'4"   Weight: 170
Origin: International Free Agent, 2013

The Report: Eligible by only eight innings, Alcantara has one of the most electric arms we'll cover this list cycle. His fastball sits in the mid-90s, can touch triple digits, and moves with wiffle-ball run and sink. Alcantara also features a power slider in the upper-80s that falls off the deck with late tilt. His changeup can be too firm, low-90s and just a bit of a runner, but it will flash good sink when he has feel for it. There's also a show-me curve he uses sparingly.

The stuff all comes free and easy from a fairly compact delivery. For a batter, an inning, sometimes even a start, Alcantara can look like a true front-of-the-rotation arm, but he struggles to command his stuff consistently. In part, that's because everything moves so much. The fastball can miss armside just because of the sheer amount of run. It's also not entirely clear that he knows where everything is going. Sometimes that means it's center cut at 96, and other times it means he's walking guys on four pitches. The command and third pitch issues might be mitigated some in the pen—that's always been a strong possibility for the profile—but the Marlins have every reason to let Alcantara figure it out in the rotation over the next couple seasons. The fallback late-inning role will still be there, and the rewards in the rotation could be significant.

The Risks: Low. He might not be a starter long term, but Alcantara has major-league stuff and should spend all of 2019 somewhere on the Marlins staff.

Bret Sayre's Fantasy Take: It's a tale as old as time. Probable starter with great stuff seeks consistent command. You know what to expect by now. There's about a 20 percent change Alcantara harnesses the stuff enough to be a strong SP3. There's about a 40 percent chance he's a starting pitcher who gets streamed at home in shallower leagues. There's about a 20 percent chance he's a closer, and, well, you don't care about the rest, really. Best realistic scenario is a 3.50 ERA with a strikeout per inning and a WHIP slightly better than shade-your-eyes level.

3 Monte Harrison   OF   OFP: 60   Likely: 50   ETA: 2020
Born: 08/10/95   Age: 23   Bats: R   Throws: R   Height: 6'3"   Weight: 220
Origin: Round 2, 2014 Draft (#50 overall)

The Report: Double-A was always going to be a tough test for Harrison after his breakout 2017 season. The premium athleticism is still present, but less of a carrying tool in the upper minors. Not that it hurts mind you; Harrison is a plus runner with a plus arm and he can still outrun any mistakes he might make with routes and reads in center. His raw power bumps the top of the scale now that he's filled out, and he has the kind of baseball body that makes our dear, departed Craig Goldstein mutter "hardware" involuntarily. All good so far, very good even.

The stat line above isn't egregiously bad for a still little-bit-raw prospect in his first season in Double-A. But here's the thing: Harrison struck out 215 times last season. That's... a lot. We've become a little inured to high K-rates in this era, and when you hit the ball as hard as Harrison does, a 30% K-rate might be manageable. Or, it would in the majors; this is 37% in the minors. A lot of it stems from timing issues, as Harrison tends to drift forward early in his swing and get out of sync. He also has issues recognizing quality spin as well. The athletic tools give him a floor, but if you want a picture of how it might go bad at the highest level, look no further than a guy he was traded with, Lewis Brinson. I'm going to float Harrison for another year because the tools are so loud (and I tend to be enamored with this profile like with, uh, Lewis Brinson), but the bust risk is real.

The Risks: High. On the one hand, Harrison has a broad base of athletic skills and he'll be an above-average defensive center fielder. With that as a baseline, he won't have to hit that much to have some sort of major league career. On the other hand, he struck out 215 times in the Southern League.

Bret Sayre's Fantasy Take: Congrats to those of you who traded Harrison away after his breakout 2017 season. Condolences to those of you who didn't. The speed is still the selling point, and Harrison has long had the baserunning acumen to match, which could help him push 25-30 steals in the majors. The power will be dampened a little by his home park, but not nearly as much as the wind power he generates at the plate. If he's a 20/20 guy with a .220 average, that's likely a borderline top-40 outfielder, and makes Harrison a very borderline top-101 dynasty prospect.

4. Isan Diaz 2B

OFP: 60   Likely: 50   ETA: Late 2019
Born: 05/27/96   Age: 23   Bats: L   Throws: R   Height: 5'10"   Weight: 185
Origin: Round 2, 2014 Draft (#70 overall)

The Report: The package the Marlins got back for Christian Yelich was "high-variance" as top prospect packages go, and the Fish generally got the short end of the production projection in 2018. Diaz arguably had the best overall performance with the stick, but he also has the least defensive value—average second baseman—while both Brinson and Harrison could be plus center fielders. So there will be more pressure generally on Diaz's bat, and there was actually plenty to like this year, even if the top line numbers won't wow you.

Diaz offers plus raw power from a relatively compact swing. There's enough muscle and lift to it that he can get beat in the zone, but he has a decent approach at the plate and better bat control than you'd think. He's strong enough to dump hits into the outfield off his mistakes, and while he's likely to be Three-True-

Outcomish, there's a decent shot at a solid-average hit tool due to the quality of his contact. In the field, Diaz gets it done. He isn't the slickest fielder in the world, but the actions and arm are fine for the keystone.

The Risks: High. Upper minors arms didn't show much mercy for this Diaz brother, and the swing-and-miss might never allow enough of the raw power into games to carry a starting role.

Bret Sayre's Fantasy Take: Diaz's time as a fantasy-relevant prospect has outlasted the TINO Podcast, on which Mauricio Rubio fawned over him on multiple occasions as a teenager. Now older and seemingly less interesting, just like the rest of us, Diaz is on the cusp of being lineup ready. Don't let the prospect fatigue get to you. For my money, Diaz is the second-best fantasy prospect in this system and has the power/speed potential of Harrison on the infield and without the extreme strikeout rate.

5. Nick Neidert   RHP

OFP: 55   Likely: 50   ETA: Late 2019
Born: 11/20/96   Age: 22   Bats: R   Throws: R   Height: 6'1"   Weight: 180
Origin: Round 2, 2015 Draft (#60 overall)

The Report: Welcome to the "pitchability righty" portion of the list. Neidert has a bit of funk and deception in his delivery, and it looks almost like he's throwing darts up there. He's no baz on the mound though, as Neidert has above-average command of his low-90s fastball. It's a heavy fastball and there is some tail and riding life when he elevates it. His best secondary is an above-average change that fades and sinks, and it plays to grade in part because he maintains his armspeed on the pitch.

Neidert's slider has improved this year and gives him a swing-and-miss option against righties. It can get a little slurvy, but there's good two-plane action when he stays on top of it and gets it down and out of the zone. He can also backdoor it to lefties. Neidert's curve is below-average, a humpy 12-6 that tends to show a bit early, but gives him another look to steal a strike with here and there. Despite the unorthodox delivery, he is a strike thrower, although the best pitch here is a 55, and he will have fine margins with his command against the best hitters in the world.

The Risks: Low. While Neidert may not offer the most potential impact of the arms on this list, he's pitched well in the upper minors. These profiles aren't safe per se—sometimes the pitchability dudes without a clear plus offering get Aaron Blair'd—but Neidert is major-league-ready and can get you out in a few different ways.

Bret Sayre's Fantasy Take: Welcome to five years of fantasy experts telling you that Neidert is a great matchups guy against crappy teams at home. They'll also spell his name "N-i-e-d-e-r-t" at least 20 percent of the time.

6 **Connor Scott OF** OFP: 55   Likely: 45   ETA: 2022
Born: 10/08/99   Age: 19   Bats: L   Throws: L   Height: 6'4"   Weight: 180
Origin: Round 1, 2018 Draft (#13 overall)

The Report: I get Mickey Moniak vibes from Scott, which makes for an interesting comp. It doesn't realllllllllly fit the profile, mind you. Scott is taller, much more physical, more projectable, less likely to stick in center field, much less polished with the stick. There are some similarities with the swing though: They both bail out at times and get a little long and hitchy with the hand path. They are both plus runners, although Scott is more likely to fill out and slow down and he's looked lost in center field at times.

We at the BP Prospect Team have always contended that the problem with Moniak the prospect—well other than the lack of production or projection so far—was that he went 1.1. If he had gone, say, 13th overall like Scott, the conversation around him would be different. But the "1.1 prep outfielder" has a connotation. Scott even looks that part more, one could argue. It's a classic projectable frame with some plus tools. He'll flash really loud contact at times. The swing is more geared for power too. The rawness against A-ball arms is more acceptable for the 13th overall pick.

In each case, the underlying problem is the same: Both just need to hit more. Scott didn't have the plus-plus projection on the hit tool coming out of the showcase circuit, which makes his production thus far seem less dire. Before this turns into "What we talk about when we talk about prep outfielders," Scott isn't the same prospect Moniak was post-draft, but they may both end up fourth outfielders in the end. Only one will be considered a true draft disappointment when that happens.

The Risks: Extreme. Scott is a polarizing prospect with variance way beyond his written OFP/Likely here. He may not hit at all (and hasn't so far). He may end up in a corner. He may grow into a plus regular. We likely won't know for a while.

Bret Sayre's Fantasy Take: It's far easier for dynasty owners to take the risk on prospects like Scott because there are always more coming. In a deep 2018 dynasty draft class, Scott has the tools of someone who should be taken in the back of the first round, and while the (very) early returns weren't super encouraging, he'll be 19 for all of the 2019 season and will get to grow into full-season ball. There's five-tool potential here and an OF2 ceiling to boot.

7 **Zac Gallen RHP** OFP: 55   Likely: 45   ETA: 2019
Born: 08/03/95   Age: 23   Bats: R   Throws: R   Height: 6'2"   Weight: 191
Origin: Round 3, 2016 Draft (#106 overall)

The Report: I'd be tempted to cut-and-paste the Neidert report here, but there are a few subtle differences in the profiles. Gallen works primarily off a fastball/cutter combo that sit either side of 90 mph. The lean righty is a good athlete who repeats his delivery well. His upright landing and near-OTT slot gives the fastball some plane, and you'll occasionally see some armside wiggle as well.

Gallen has above-average command of both the fastball and cutter and is quite effective when working down in the zone. The fastball can be a bit hittable up, where it tends to flatten out. The cutter works well off the fastball and features late, tight tilt. He rounds out his arsenal with a fringy change and curve. Four offerings either side of average and above-average command is not the most exciting profile, but Gallen has had success all the way up the ladder, and the cutter should miss enough bats to make him an effective backend starter.

The Risks: Low. While Gallen may not offer the most potential impact of the arms on this list, he's pitched well in the upper minors. These profiles aren't safe per se—sometimes the pitchability dudes without a clear plus offering get Aaron Blair'd—but Gallen is major-league-ready and can get you out in a few different ways.

Bret Sayre's Fantasy Take: There have been pitchers like this who have turned into mixed-league types, but odds are Gallen simply ends up as a solid NL-only starter, who is just slightly outpacing the stronger setup relievers in fantasy value. The short-term opportunity is there in Miami as well. Also, just like Aaron Blair, Gallen will always be a lefty to me.

8. Jorge Guzman   RHP   OFP: 55   Likely: 45

ETA: 2020; could move quickly with spring pen conversion.
Born: 01/28/96   Age: 23   Bats: R   Throws: R   Height: 6'2"   Weight: 182
Origin: International Free Agent, 2014

The Report: Guzman was the main piece in the Giancarlo Stanton trade last winter, and his first year in full-season ball likely wasn't good enough to dissuade people that it was a salary dump on the Marlins part. But if you catch Guzman on the right day, you'll wonder how anyone squares him up (and on the wrong day, you'll wonder why anyone swings at all). The elite velocity is still there, as Guzman sat in the upper-90s as a starter and routinely touched triple digits. Despite the easy cheese, his command and movement are both below-average. His arm action is compact and quick, but the fastball comes out with all the accuracy of a toddler holding a firehose.

Guzman's best secondary is a power breaker in the mid-80s that flashes plus, but the feel and shape will come and go. He offers a firm change that touches 90 as well. This is a standard power right-handed relief arsenal, but we don't know yet if the control will play better in short bursts. He'll be 23 in 2019 and hasn't pitched in the upper minors yet, so there's more uncertainty than you'd want in this profile.

The Risks: High. Given Guzman's stuff and age you'd expect him to have been more dominant in the Florida State League, and he's a high probability reliever where 100 mph isn't as special as it once was.

Bret Sayre's Fantasy Take: There's way more name recognition with Guzman than actual dynasty value, so if you can get something useful for him, I'd advise it. The odds of him surviving into the majors as a half-decent starter are low.

9 **Jordan Yamamoto   RHP**   OFP: 55   Likely: 45   ETA: 2020
Born: 05/11/96   Age: 23   Bats: R   Throws: R   Height: 6'0"   Weight: 185
Origin: Round 12, 2014 Draft (#356 overall)

The Report: Back to the low-90s we go with Yamamoto, although he posted a better K-rate than Guzman in 2018 with his array of average-to-solid-average stuff. Yamamoto is adept at spotting his fastball armside and there is a bit of wiggle that way as well. He'll work all four quadrants with the pitch, but it's a bit more hittable than you'd like if he isn't painting the corners.

You could make a case for the slider or change as his best secondary. The slider is more heavily-used and will flash plus, but it doesn't always invite chases gloveside due to his inconsistent command of it. It won't always show ideal depth either given his lower slot. Yamamoto often has good feel for the change, and there's a bit of fade to it, but it's not a true "pull the string" offering yet. He also throws a big, loopy curve which can dip into the upper-60s. It gives a different eye line and velo band for the hitters, but he has trouble manipulating its shape and location.

Yamamoto doesn't have an obvious bat-misser here, but he'll throw anything in any count. You can ding him for his height as well; the track record for short righties throwing in the low-90s is neither long nor inspiring, but he's another "greater-than-the-sum-of-his-parts" dude in this system. You'd bet on one of them working out at least?

The Risks: Medium. Yamamoto is a polished righty in the mold of Neidert and Gallen, but he has a longer injury history and a shorter track record of success in the upper minors.

Bret Sayre's Fantasy Take: There's some buzz around Yamamoto from his strong performance in the AFL, but he's still a poor bet to be more than an SP5 at peak, even with Marlins Park backing him. If he has a few seasons along the lines of the one Marco Gonzales just put up (don't laugh, Gonzales was a top-50 starter), it'll be a highly successful outcome.

10 **Braxton Garrett   LHP**   OFP: 55   Likely: 45   ETA: 2022
Born: 08/05/97   Age: 21   Bats: L   Throws: L   Height: 6'3"   Weight: 190
Origin: Round 1, 2016 Draft (#7 overall)

Miami Marlins 2019

The Report: "This space left intentionally blank" is not really going to fly in this format, but we don't have anything new to add to the Garrett report after he missed all of 2018 recovering from Tommy John surgery. He was one of my favorite arms in the 2016 draft, but that was two years ago, and he's made exactly four professional starts. The fastball wasn't overwhelming before the surgery, and his plus command projection may take awhile to come back after the surgery. There was a potential plus-plus curve that got him drafted in the top ten. Will it come back? We'll have a better idea next year. All of this is to say that I'm basically blindfolded and throwing a dart for rankings/role purposes here. Perhaps there is some merit to John Sickels throwing a C+ on all these TJ guys until they are back on a mound. Regardless, we seem to be writing more and more of them lately.

The Risks: Extreme. He still hasn't thrown a pitch in a live game since the Tommy John surgery, so the stuff/projection is still an open-ended question until 2019.

Bret Sayre's Fantasy Take: Garrett is an interesting name to keep an eye on in deep formats (think 250-300 prospects deep), as a return to form post-TJ could shoot him back up to a top-150-or-so dynasty prospect at this time next year. Just don't waste the roster spot yet.

The Next Five:

11 **Trevor Rogers   LHP**
Born: 11/13/97   Age: 21   Bats: L   Throws: L   Height: 6'6"   Weight: 185
Origin: Round 1, 2017 Draft (#13 overall)

The Marlins went back to the lefty prep pitcher well in the 2017 draft. Unlike Garrett, Rogers did pitch in 2018, but his results were poor. Is it fair to penalize bad performance more than no performance? Perhaps not, but Rogers confirmed a lot of the concerns I had about him as an amateur. Despite being a lefty projection bet, he's already 20 and still won't consistently show plus fastball velocity. Both secondaries—a change and a slurvy slider—remain below average, and it will take some squinting and a fair bit of projection to get them to 5s. "Tall pitcher" command issues remain. Rogers is still a project with some upside, but there's been little progress on the deliverables so far.

12 **Brian Miller   OF**
Born: 08/20/95   Age: 23   Bats: L   Throws: R   Height: 6'1"   Weight: 186
Origin: Round 1, 2017 Draft (#36 overall)

There will be a lot of speedy, no-pop center field blurbs in the coming months. It's a continuum from 101 guys (The Manuel Margots and Magneuris Sierras) to the bench outfielders; I need to pad some of these lesser systems out to 6,000 words or so.

The underlying skill set won't change much. There will be below-average power (Miller has one home run in 185 career games). There will be above-average run times, plus centerfield glove projections, and then the question will be "how much will he actually hit?" We are not always great at divining this (see... uh, Manuel Margot and Magneuris Sierra), and this is not merely an excuse to spout one of my favorite mantras: "The hardest thing to project is the major-league hit tool." Okay, it's a little bit that, but this profile is specifically tricky due to the complete lack of power.

Miller has a very high contact rate now, but how good is that contact against premium stuff? If he's a .250 hitter, he's an up and down guy. If he's a .300 hitter, maybe he's Ben Revere. That's a hit a week, as Bull Durham taught us, "one groundball with eyes." Miller has the kind of inside-out, oppo-geared swing endemic to this profile, and you worry about the bat getting knocked out of his hands in the majors. The production already took a bit of a dip in Double-A. Sometimes you are just Zack Granite (sigh, I should probably double check his list eligibility).

13 Will Banfield   C
Born: 11/18/99   Age: 19   Bats: R   Throws: R   Height: 6'0"   Weight: 200
Origin: Round 2, 2018 Draft (#69 overall)

A nice get in the second round of this year's draft, Banfield was regarded by some as the best prep catcher in the 2018 draft. You probably know how I feel about that general profile by now, but I will just mention that I have already made several unsuccessful attempts at repurposing boygenius lyrics for a player blurb ("Prep catcher in the rear view mirror / hasn't caught a thing yet / Batting practice souvenirs / Anything's worth trying").

Banfield breaks the usual mold a bit here due to his advanced defensive skills. He has plus arm strength, good footwork, a quick transfer, and polished receiving skills for his experience level. Although he's on the slender side for the position at present, there's the outline of the catcher body here—mostly in the butt. Instead the questions here are about the bat. Banfield has some pop—his first three hits in the Sally league were all bombs, but there's length and leverage to get it. There is substantial swing-and-miss risk here, but both the bat and glove have plenty of time to develop since you won't see Banfield in the majors until about the time the third boygenius album drops (one can hope).

14 Bryson Brigman   SS
Born: 06/19/95   Age: 24   Bats: R   Throws: R   Height: 5'11"   Weight: 180
Origin: Round 3, 2016 Draft (#87 overall)

Having multiple ex-Mariners prospects dotting this list may speak to how far the Marlins still have to go with this rebuild, but Brigman started to show a bit with the stick to go with his slick glove. Acquired from Seattle as part of the Cameron

Miami Marlins 2019

Maybin deal, Brigman is an above-average defender with good range and enough arm to make most of the throws at the 6. He's more grinder than quick-twitch, but he has a good enough first step, above-average speed, and gets it done on the dirt.

Brigman finally started to hit for average this year as a 23-year-old in High-A, which might raise an eyebrow or two, but the profile at the plate supports it. He's a pesky type that prioritizes line-drive contact over power. He works oppo primarily, but can sting a ball pull-side now and again. Brigman profiles best as a fifth infielder due to the lack of game power and lingering questions about his bat against better pitching, but there's a non-zero chance he can be a table-setting middle infielder for a second-division team… like, say, the Marlins.

15 Jose Devers SS
Born: 12/07/99   Age: 19   Bats: L   Throws: R   Height: 6'0"   Weight: 155
Origin: International Free Agent, 2016

Brigman and Devers make a neatly matched pair at the end of our ordinal rankings as glove-first middle infielders. Devers is a better defender—a clear everyday shortstop with the leather. He's a better runner as well, but the bat is less advanced and he's shown even less raw power than Brigman. Devers has also been young for his levels, so if you want to try and squint and see some projection in the bat through your age-relative-to-league colored glasses, we won't stop you. There's even a bit of physical projection left, although he's likely to always be on the skinny side; Rafael got all the Big Boy SZN genes in the family. You'd be forgiven for thinking that Jose fell off the Cesar Izturis family tree.

Others of note:

Tristan Pompey, OF, Advanced-A Jupiter
On the other hand, the Marlins third round pick—and Dalton's brother—didn't fall far from the family tree. A switch-hitting, quick twitch outfielder with fringe power projection, the younger Pompey handled his fairly aggressive A-ball assignments without issue. While a small sample, it was still a positive signpost after his poor showing with wood on the Cape the previous summer. He's susceptible to spin, and there's swing and miss issues generally, but if he can stay healthier than Dalton, he should slot into a bench outfielder role fairly quickly.

Joe Dunand, SS, Low-A Greensboro
Falling even in the same zip code as the A-Rod family tree would be a boon to any baseball prospect, though Dunand—Rodriguez's nephew—is more Brian-Anderson-lite than Alex-Rodriguez-lite. He's a shortstop for now, though his frame and limited range will shift him over to third base where the arm and glove

will play as solid-average. Dunand struggled badly in his first taste of Double-A, but if he can get to enough of his plus raw power in games he could be a fringy third base option or corner infield bench bat.

Victor Mesa, OF, Did not play

Opportunities to see the 17-year-old play have been limited even by Cuban mystery player standards. I can tell you that he has a projectable body and a nice swing from the left side, but this has the look of an obvious package deal, with Victor Jr. along for the ride with Victor Victor (even though those are supposed to be banned). As we wrote when the Mesas signed, it's not even clear just yet whether the Marlins are going to have Victor Jr. hit from both sides or just the left. Truth be told, we wouldn't be writing him up here if he hadn't signed at the same time as his more regarded brother. He'll probably play in a complex league and we're likely a year or two away from even knowing if he's a few years away.

Top Talents 25 and Under (born 4/1/93 or later):

1. Victor Victor Mesa
2. Sandy Alcantara
3. Lewis Brinson
4. Brian Anderson
5. Trevor Richards
6. Monte Harrison
7. Isan Diaz
8. Nick Neidert
9. Magneuris Sierra
10. Connor Scott

I'll be honest and say that I don't have the slightest idea what to do with Lewis Brinson here; I can make the case for virtually any spot in the top ten. We've ranked him as a top 20 prospect in baseball for the last three years, but because of his swing length and pitch recognition issues there was always an unusually high delta in the hit tool for his ranks and levels. More than we'd have liked, there was some risk that he wouldn't hit.

Here today, it really, really looks like Brinson just can't hit major-league pitching; he has nearly a full season of combined playing time in the majors where he's hit .189 with 24 walks to 137 strikeouts. I can't even tell you that he's looked any better than that, because he hasn't. The other four tools still show up enough, but you can't steal first base. He's needed adjustment time before and came out the other side, and a summer hip problem is just enough of an injury excuse to give him a chance to re-run it all, so I'm hesitant to declare all hope lost and send him spiraling down quite as far as I sent Sierra. But I sure wouldn't make him the centerpiece of a Christian Yelich trade again, either.

Brian Anderson entered 2018 as a defense-first third baseman with raw power but questions about his overall hitting. He proceeded to spend much of the season in right field to accommodate, uh, Martin Prado and Miguel Rojas, and he put together an above-average offensive campaign that, in a down year for newcomers, might have won him the Rookie of the Year Award. The Marlins finally let Anderson settle in at third in August, and you'd think they'd just roll him out there for the next couple years. Alas, Prado is probably going to be back in 2019; sometimes paychecks drive decisions over player development. Anderson is already 25 and 2018 might be his peak if the power never spikes, but he's already a pretty nifty player.

We never put Trevor Richards on a prospect list here at Baseball Prospectus. He pitched four years at Division II Drury University, and even though any vaguely promising senior now gets popped for a small bonus in the draft for bonus manipulation these days, he went undrafted multiple times. Before entering organized baseball, he spent parts of two seasons in the independent Frontier League. He signed with the Marlins in the middle of 2016, initially to fill a bullpen spot in the short-season New York-Penn League. Just a season-and-a-half later, he won the Marlins fifth starter job out of camp, held it for most of the season, and struck out more than a batter per inning working off a dominant changeup. His fastball and breaking ball both remain fringy, but it's a hell of a change, and DRA thinks he was even better in 2018 than the traditional rates do. So we'll take our last best chance to plug him to the world on a list before he graduates with Anderson.

Magneuris Sierra had a nightmare season. There's no way to sugarcoat how bad he was: he compiled the fifth-worst position player WARP in the majors in just 156 plate appearances, and he didn't hit in Triple-A at all either. It was his age-22 season, so there's some time to recover, and he has enough secondary skills with his defensive prowess and speed to provide some reserve value even if the offense never rebounds. Yet he's in even more danger than Brinson of being lapped on the organizational depth chart.

With Brinson, Harrison, Sierra, and Guzman all running into roadblocks on the path to success, and nobody particularly making a leap in the other direction, we'd be remiss not to point out that the return on the Jeter-led firesale of Miami's incumbent MLB stars looks far worse today than it did last winter. Then again, accumulating talent was never the point there, was it?

Part 3: Featured Articles

The Hole in The Shift is Fixing Itself

Russell Carleton

I've been on a bit of a mission against The Shift of late. I'm not out to get The Shift for the usual reasons that people oppose it. The words "the right way to play the game" won't be found on my lips. If a team wants to pursue a strategy that is within the rules and it works, then by all means, they have my blessing (not that they need it). Instead, my concern with The Shift is a worry that it doesn't work, or at least that it has a flaw that needs fixing.

The data show that while The Shift does a decent job of preventing singles on balls in play (what it's supposed to do), it also increases the number of walks that happen in front of it, and the number of additional walks outweighs the number of singles saved. It's a problem because you can't throw a guy out if he gets to walk to first base.

But the "why" was important. It seemed that The Shift was changing the way in which pitchers pitched. We saw that there were fewer fastballs thrown in front of The Shift than we might otherwise expect, and that pitchers tended to stay out of the strike zone a little more. Not by a lot. In fact, it might not even be visible to the naked eye. The percentage of pitches that are out of the zone goes from 51.0 to 53.3 from a standard defense (two right/two left) to a full shift (three on one side). That difference stands up even after we control for the types of hitters that get shifted against. And it's enough to drive up the walk rate to where it cancels out the benefits that teams thought they were getting with The Shift… and then some.

But there was some hope. I found that when individual pitchers stayed closer to the in-zone/out-of-zone mix that they used without The Shift on, they could still get the benefits of The Shift without the walk problems. So, in theory, a team could simply figure out a way to convince its pitchers to not fall prey to the walk trap and The Shift would once again be their friend.

It's reasonable to think that some teams might be more hip to this idea than others. Maybe some figured it out a year before the others. Maybe they were better at getting the message across to their pitchers. Or, maybe no one has figured it out yet.

Warning! Gory Mathematical Details Ahead!

I used data from 2015-2017, made available through MLB's data portal, Baseball Savant. They are kind enough to note when teams are using an infield shift (three fielders on one side of second base), as opposed to a "strategic shift" (someone's playing a bit out of position, but it's not quite that drastic) or a "standard" alignment.

Since we're doing this by team, I can't just look at raw walk rates, because we know that some teams have good pitchers and others have not-so-good pitchers. Some have a mix of both. I used the log-odds ratio method to take into account a batter's general walking proclivities, and a pitcher's as well, and then shoving them into a binary logistic regression. Then, I asked the computer to generate a specific coefficient for each team's pitchers, for when they went into The Shift and how that affected their walk rate.

Using those coefficients, I was able to project what would happen if a league-average pitcher faced a league-average hitter (which we expect would product a league-average walk rate; from 2015-2017, 7.7 percent of plate appearances ended in a walk) and then just switched his hat. Here's the top five and the bottom five:

Top 5 Teams	Projected Shift Walk Rate	Bottom 5 Teams	Projected Shift Walk Rate
Rockies	6.2%	Rangers	11.2%
Pirates	6.7%	Mets	10.4%
Indians	7.2%	Dodgers	10.2%
Astros	7.3%	Cardinals	9.9%
Braves	7.7%	Tigers	9.7%

There are probably people out there right now trying to figure out what the common thread is among the top and bottom teams. I'm sure, because this is Baseball Prospectus, people are already trying to make the case that sabermetric "early adopters" have some sort of edge here. I think that the more interesting piece is that by the time you get to fifth place in The Shift, we're at league average.

As a sanity check, I examined the issue on a pitch-by-pitch level, looking at how often pitchers threw their pitches in the GameDay strike zone, and again using the same basic methodology and getting team-specific coefficients. The names on the list re-arranged themselves, but the idea was the same, and the two lists correlated with an R of .593.

There's a reason that I don't usually do this type of leaderboard post. I don't really know what the Rockies, Pirates, Indians, Astros, and Braves have in common, or what they have that the bottom five don't. I can put a shrug emoji here and say, "Well, it must be something!" but that seems like a cop-out. Instead, I'd like to present another table and suggest that the table above doesn't even really matter anymore.

Year	League Percent Outside K Zone (Full Shift)	League Percent in K Zone (No Shift)	Difference
2015	54.1%	51.1%	3.0%
2016	53.3%	50.9%	2.4%
2017	52.6%	50.9%	1.7%
2018	52.0%	50.7%	1.3%

The hole in The Shift is fixing itself, and it's coming down really fast league wide. In my earlier work on The Shift, I suggested that until teams stopped having such a huge difference between their out-of-zone rate with and without The Shift on, there would just be too many walks for The Shift to make sense. It seems that all 30 of them have been working toward just that. I once estimated that it takes about 10 years for an idea to filter its way through baseball. At this rate, it looks like teams are going to catch up a lot faster than that. And yeah, they're all saber-smart now.

It's likely that whatever magic it was that the Rockies and Pirates had has made its way to Texas and Queens. Or is at least on its way. And if teams are committing to fixing the walk problem, then it's likely that they will continue shifting and shifting a lot.

And eventually it's going to actually make sense for them to do it.

—Russell Carleton is a former author of Baseball Prospectus and now an analyst for the New York Mets.

The State of the Quality Start

Rob Mains

One of the seven things you (probably) didn't know about the 2018 season is that quality starts—defined as a start lasting six or more innings with three or fewer earned runs allowed—as a percentage of total starts cratered to an all-time low of 41 percent. I want to look a little more deeply into this, since it's been a while (May of 2016, to be exact) since I've examined quality starts.

The term *quality start* is credited to *Philadelphia Inquirer* sportswriter John Lowe. It's been derided ever since he coined it in December of 1985. Three runs in six innings? That's a 4.50 ERA! In what world is that a measure of quality?

Let's start with that criticism. It's true that 3 x 9 / 6 = 4.5. (You came here for this sort of high-level math, right?) But it's also true that type of start, meeting the bare minimum for earning a quality start, is unusual. Here's the proportion of quality starts in which the pitcher lasted exactly six innings and yielded exactly three earned runs. (I'm going to confine this analysis to the 30-team era, 1998-present. Almost all data retrieved in this article is via the Baseball-Reference Play Index.)

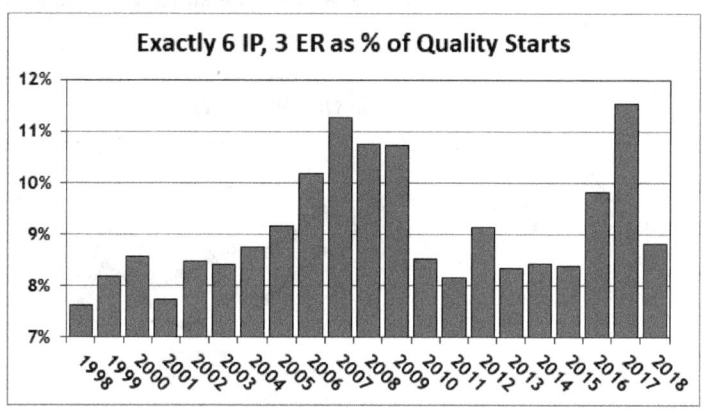

There were 1,997 quality starts in 2018. Only 176, or fewer than one in 11, featured a pitcher going six innings and allowing three earned runs. Put another way, the percentage of quality starts that resulted in a 4.50 ERA (8.8 percent) is less than half the percentage of games in which a batter hit two home runs and his team lost (22.5 percent; 237-69 won-lost). That doesn't impugn hitting two homers.

So if a 4.50 ERA isn't the norm, what is? How good are quality starts?

Pretty good, it turns out. First, on a team level:

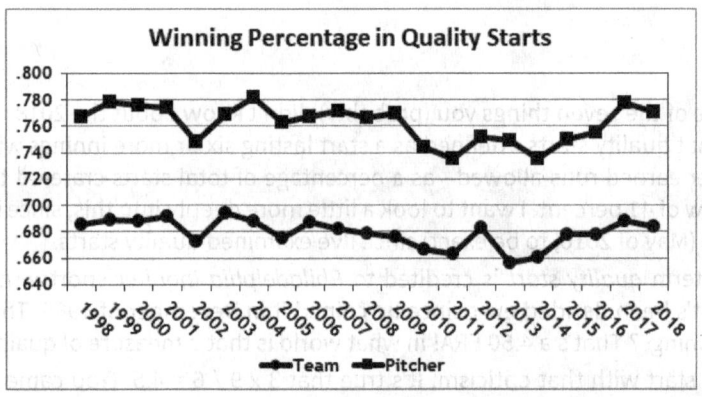

Teams receiving a quality start from their pitcher won 68.4 percent of their games in 2018, in line with the 30-team era average of 67.9 percent. A team with a .684 winning percentage wins 111 games. Getting a quality start is definitely a good thing. Individual pitchers throwing quality starts have a higher winning percentage because a big slice of team losses is assigned to a reliever.

If teams do well in quality starts, how well do the starting pitchers do? Again, very well.

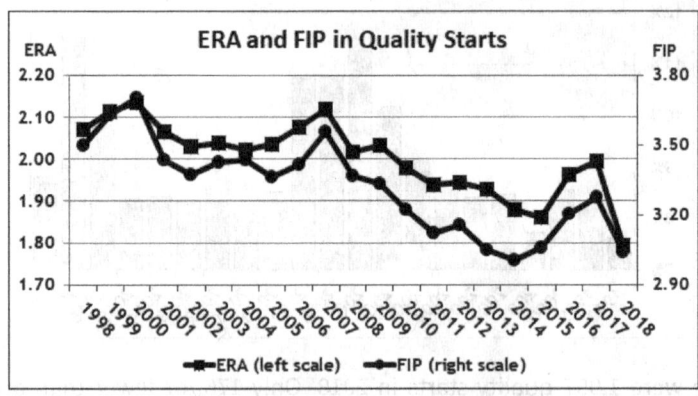

Pitchers in quality starts had a 1.79 ERA (blue line) in 2018, *the lowest in the 30-team era*. Their FIP was higher, 3.04, but still excellent. In the 30-team era, only 2014 had a lower FIP for quality starts, 3.01.

But, of course, the run environment in 2014 was different. Teams in 2014 scored 4.07 runs per game, the fewest in a non-strike year since 1976. They scored 4.45 runs per game in 2018. So surrendering a 3.04 FIP in 2018 is more impressive than 3.01 in 2014. Accordingly, let's look at ERA and FIP in quality starts relative to league averages.

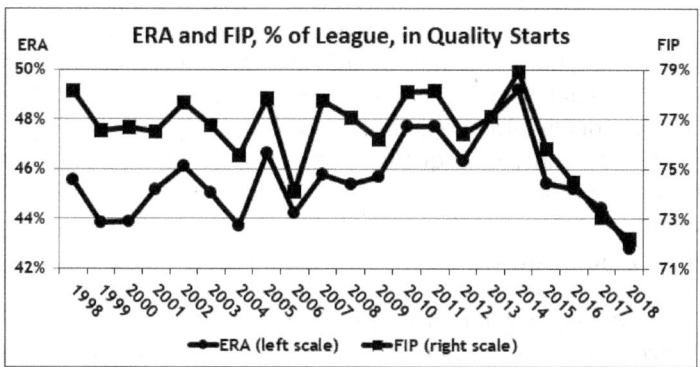

This tells a more dramatic story. Starting pitchers in 2018 gave up a 4.19 ERA and a 4.21 FIP. Starters in quality starts gave up a 1.79 ERA, 43 percent of the league average. Starters in quality starts gave up a 3.04 FIP, 72 percent of the league average. Both of these marks represent lows in the 30-team era.

The takeaway here is this: *Quality starts are better, relative to other starts, than they've ever been over the past 21 years.*

Maybe during the winter I'll look at this over a longer arc of time. For now, though, we can definitively say quality starts are the best they've ever been since the Diamondbacks and Rays joined the majors.

Yet, paradoxically, they're down.

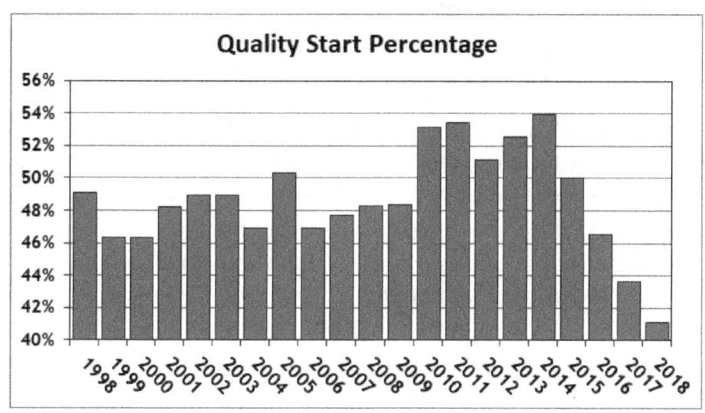

This graph covers only the 30-team era. In my article last week, though, I looked at the years 1908-2018. The result was the same. The 41 percent of starts in 2018 that were quality starts are an all-time low, well below the runners-up: 1930's 43 percent (the year teams scored an all-time record 5.55 runs per game) and last year's 44 percent.

The normal explanation for a dip in quality start percentage is an increase in scoring. When teams score a lot of runs, it's harder for starting pitchers to last six or more innings and limit opponents to three earned runs. From 1998 to 2014, the correlation between runs scored per game and the percentage of starts that were quality starts was -0.94. That means there was an extremely close relationship: More runs, fewer quality starts. Too small a sample? Go back to the start of the Expansion Era, 1961, and the relationship is even more negative, a -0.95 correlation, though 2014.

But that's broken down over the past four years:

- 2015: Runs per game increased from 4.07 to 4.25, quality start percentage decreased from 54.0 to 50.1. Yes, that's a negative relationship, but the regression model would predict a decline of 1.5 percentage points. We got 3.9 instead.
- 2016: Runs per game increased from 4.25 to 4.48, quality start percentage decreased from 50.1 to 46.6. Past experience would suggest a decline of just 1.8 percentage points. We got 3.4.
- 2017: Runs per game increased from 4.48 to 4.65, quality start percentage decreased from 46.6 to 43.6. Again, the direction's right, but the magnitude isn't. Using the relationship from 1998 to 2014, that increase in scoring should've reduced quality starts by 1.3 percentage points, not 2.9.
- 2018: Runs per game declined from 4.65 to 4.45. That should've resulted in the quality start percentage moving in the other direction, rising 1.6 points. It didn't. It fell 2.6 points, as noted, to an all-time low.

Granted, we're talking about just four years here. Maybe they're outliers. But I don't think they are. Quality starts, as noted, are as good or better than ever. But they're rarer than ever as well. And I think I know why.

To get a quality start, you need to allow three or fewer earned and pitch at least six innings. That's 18 outs. Here's a graph showing the number of starting pitchers who limited their opponents to three or fewer earned runs but got pulled after pitching at least five innings but fewer than six:

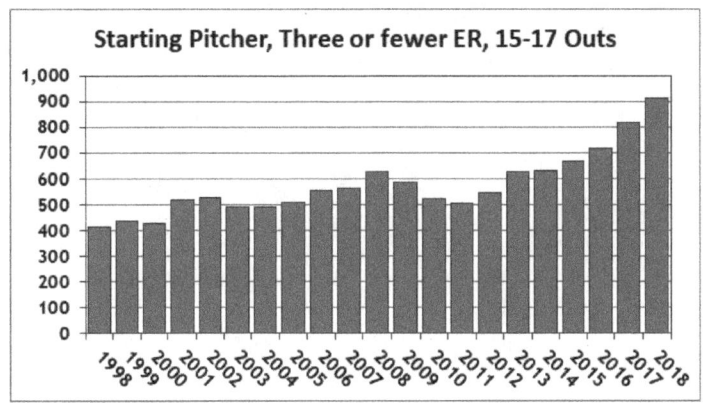

A pitcher getting 15 outs pitched five innings. A pitcher getting 16 outs pitched 5 1/3. A pitcher getting 17 outs pitched 5 2/3. More than ever before, pitchers are being removed from games in which they are within 1-3 outs of a quality start, falling just short of the six-inning finish line. Widespread acknowledgement of the times-through-the-order penalty and a flotilla of available bullpen arms is making the quality start simultaneously both more excellent and more rare.

Which is ironic, given that we saw a new post-war quality start record this season:

Rank	Pitcher	Season	Consecutive QS
1	Jacob deGrom	2018	24
2	Bob Gibson	1968	22
-	Chris Carpenter	2005	22
4	Johan Santana	2004	21
5	Luis Tiant	1968	20
-	Mike Scott	1986	20
-	Jake Arrieta	2015	20
8	Robin Roberts	1952	19
-	Tom Seaver	1973	19
-	Jack Morris	1983	19
-	Greg Maddux	1998	19
-	Josh Johnson	2010	19
-	Jon Lester	2014	19

While there have been longer streaks spread over multiple seasons, no pitcher since World War II threw more consecutive quality starts in one year than Jacob deGrom this year. The fact that he did in a year in which quality starts were the rarest they've ever been adds to the accomplishment.

—*Rob Mains is an author of Baseball Prospectus.*

Heads-Up Hacking—The First Pitch

Matthew Trueblood

Batters fell behind in a higher percentage of all plate appearances in 2018 than in any previous season for which we have pitch-by-pitch data. That kind of granular information goes back only to 1988, but we might safely assume (given all we know about baseball as it had been before that, and as it has been in the years since) that batters have *never* fallen behind at a higher rate than they did last season.

Through the 1990s, the percentage of all plate appearances that began 0-1 hovered in the high 30s and low 40s. In the 2000s, it rose steadily but slowly, through the mid-40s. In 2018, 49.8 percent of all trips to the plate began 0-1. That, as much as anything, captures in microcosm the nature of hitting in MLB today.

A countdown clock toward strike three begins ticking almost the moment a batter takes his place in the box. The league's adjusted OPS+ on the first pitch was higher in 2018 than ever before, and that has been true in most of the last 10 seasons. Batters hit .264/.289/.442 in all plate appearances in which they swung at the first pitch last season, and .241/.330/.395 in all plate appearances in which they took that first offering.

The percentage differences in batting average and isolated power there favor swinging at the first pitch by more than in any season since 1988, while the difference in on-base percentage favors taking by more than ever. If you want to get on base at a decent clip, it's a good idea to be patient, but you run the risk of missing the only chances you'll get to produce power.

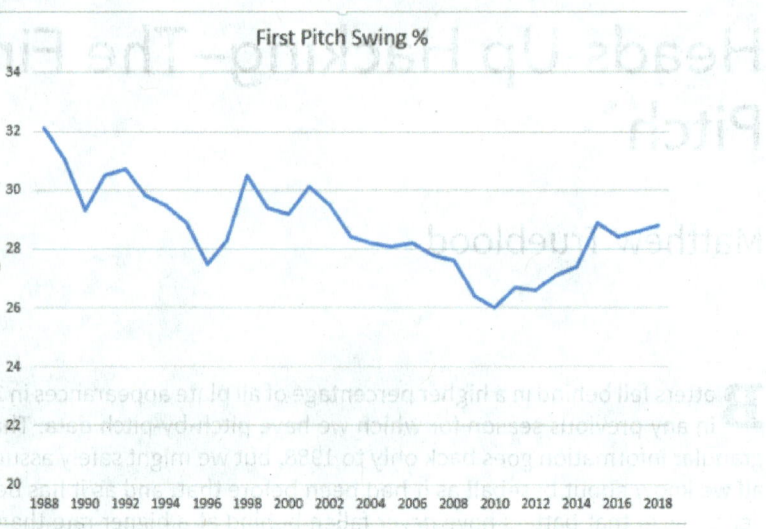

The league swung at the first pitch 28.8 percent of the time in 2018. With the isolated exception of 2015, that's the highest that number has climbed since 2002, but it might not be high enough. With the help of BP research maven Rob McQuown, I looked at the aggregate Called Strike Probability (CSProb) on the first pitch for each season since 2008, when the implementation of PITCHf/x first made measuring that possible. It's risen sharply during that period.

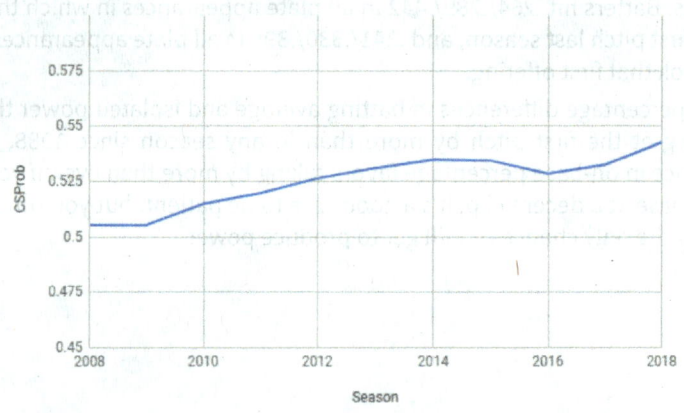

Called Strike Probability, First Pitch of PA (2008-2018)

Called Strike Probability is exactly what it sounds like: a pitch with a given CSProb has roughly that chance of being called a strike, if not swung at. In 2018, a batter who took 100 first pitches from a random sampling of the league's pitchers might expect to fall behind 54 or 55 times—up from 50 or 51 times in 2008. Almost regardless of pitch type (and, notably, especially in the case of fastballs), the first pitch tends to have more of the zone right now than ever before.

Pitchers are better at throwing strikes. They have better stuff, and believe more in their ability to miss bats within the zone. Perhaps most importantly, they know that batters are looking for one thing on the first pitch: a fastball. If they don't get it, they're likely to take the pitch. Check out how the use of sinkers and four-seamers on the first pitch has changed in a decade:

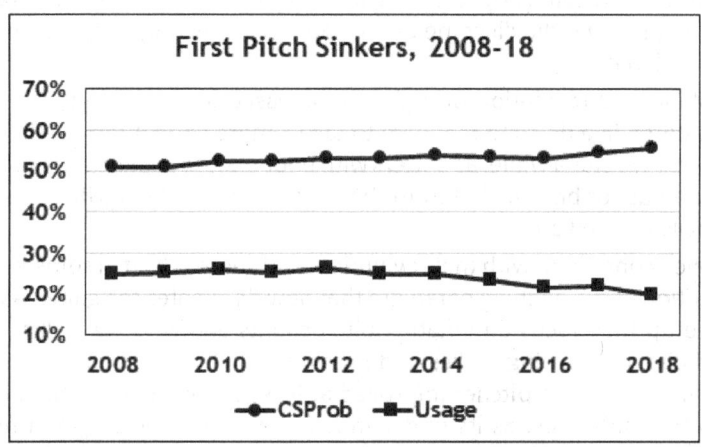

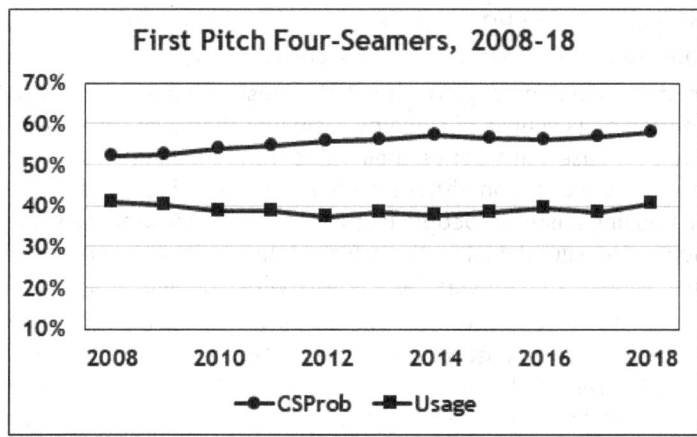

The sinker is losing its place in baseball, but the rate at which pitchers have thrown it on the first pitch hasn't dropped any faster than its usage rate in other counts. Pitchers have actually gone to their four-seamer *more* often to open counts, in the last few years, after a dip in the 2012-2015 period. What's really changed, though, and what shows up in both charts above, is that pitchers are catching more of the zone with first-pitch fastballs than they were a decade ago, or a half-decade ago. They're attacking right away, even with the pitch they know batters are expecting. The message is pretty clear: batters are being too passive.

Sliders, curves, and changeups each have more of the zone when thrown on the first pitch than they did several years ago, too, though the effect is less pronounced. Pitchers have seen the numbers; they know batters are doing better on the first pitch itself. They still feel safe throwing more and better strikes than ever before, figuring they'll come out ahead as long as they keep getting ahead to open each battle.

The Moneyball revolution brought an increased league-wide focus on OBP, which resulted in a de facto mandate to take a more patient tack at the plate. It worked very well for a while, as batters with poor plate discipline were compelled to either adjust or be expelled from the league, and pitchers with poor control were slowly weeded out.

However, concurrent with that revolution, and spurred by it in some ways, was the evolution of the pitching paradigm that now dominates the game. As batters ratcheted up their focus on inflating pitch counts and working walks, pitchers honed theirs on throwing strikes and missing bats. The league's understanding of what makes a good pitcher improved at least as much, from the mid-1990s through the mid-2000s, as its understanding of what makes a good hitter. As amphetamines and other performance-enhancing drugs were phased mostly out of the game, and as PITCHf/x broke onto the scene, individuals and teams learned how to exploit the evolved approaches of even the smartest hitters.

The ability to avoid making outs is still the most valuable one in baseball, but the magnitude of its eclipse of slugging is smaller than ever. To a greater extent than power, on-base skills derive their value from chaining—from the on-base skill levels of the players on either side of a given individual. Eleven years ago, when the housing crisis hit, people learned the hard way that the value of their homes depended a good deal on the values of their neighbors' homes. The same wasn't true, though, of their cars. So it is now, with OBP and SLG.

The global OBP in 2018 was .318. The only seasons since the Dead Ball Era in which the league got on base at a worse clip were 2013-2015, 1988, 1971-1972, and 1963-1968. This is all happening despite the aforementioned evolution of the science of hitting. It's happening despite a shift in approach and focus, one that would steer OBP ever higher, if only it were working.

Instead, it's sitting at a low ebb, and while it does so, even guys who get on base often are a little less helpful than they were 10 years ago—or 20, or 40, or 60, or 70, or 80, or 90. They're less helpful, that is, because unless there happen to be three or four other guys in the lineup who get on just as regularly, their contribution is merely to forestall the inevitable. Runs happen, increasingly, when a sudden bang happens, and that means attacking early in the count—because pitchers are sure as hell doing that.

In a league making contact on barely 75 percent of its swings, and a league in which an increasing number of pitchers can throw multiple off-speed pitches for strikes in any count, the only way to consistently generate offense is going to be aggressive. This isn't necessarily true for individuals, like Mookie Betts and Jose Ramirez, who make a lot of contact and have excellent plate discipline, and whose power comes from such natural quickness in a short stroke. Most players have to make tradeoffs, though, whether it be lowering their contact rate or raising their chase rate, in order to consistently make the quality of contact necessary to survive in today's game.

Highest %	Lowest %
Javier Baez – 48.3	Joe Mauer – 4.6
Freddie Freeman – 47.1	Mookie Betts – 9.7
Ozzie Albies – 46.3	Brett Gardner – 10.7
Jose Altuve – 44.2	Jose Ramirez – 12.0
Nick Castellanos – 44.1	Jason Kipnis – 13.8
Joey Gallo – 42.3	Jesus Aguilar – 14.5
Corey Dickerson – 40.9	Xander Bogaerts – 15.8
Salvador Perez – 40.8	Brian Dozier – 16.3
Eddie Rosario – 40.7	Mike Trout – 17.6
Nick Ahmed – 40.4	Yasmani Grandal – 17.6

Top 10 and Bottom 10 Hitters, First-Pitch Swing Rate (2018)

The question isn't which of these lists one prefers, but what they each convey, qualitatively, about the cat-and-mouse game of early-count hitting. Those top five on the left, especially, drive home the fact that for most players, getting aggressive early in the count is now key to keeping strikeout rate down and hitting for power.

For now, the message is: pitchers are coming right after batters with the nastiest stuff they've ever had. Batters had better stop giving away strike one and force hurlers to adjust, or the global OBP crisis is only going to get worse.

—*Matthew Trueblood is an author of Baseball Prospectus.*

A Hymn for the Index Stat

Patrick Dubuque

We survived without computers. I know this, because I remember the day when my dad hooked up his brand-new Atari 400 computer to the back of our 12-inch Magnavox television, and the perfect blue of the memo pad lit up for the first time. I was born just on the edge of that transitional generation, of learning cursive and balancing checkbooks and just doing math all the time, constant manual arithmetic.

It still amazes me. We learned how to sail ships without computers. We learned how to do calculus. We built towers that didn't fall down, most of the time. We engineered catapults to knock them down anyway. We built a robust system of philosophy called "utilitarianism," founded on the principle that the good of an action is evaluated by summing the effects of that action, which is the kind of formula that would make the world's mainframes crash. The whole foundation of statistics as a field is "here's math you could easily do but would die of old age first."

The fact of the matter is that there is too much math in the world to do. There are too many things changing, and too many things too small to notice, for us to handle. At some point, they become too much for the computers to handle as well, which is why we have chaos theory and undetectable earthquakes, but it's not an even fight. At some point, we fall back on intuition, and given how under-equipped we are, we're forced to bestow that intuition with some sort of supernatural superiority, the "gut feeling," that we can't prove because we can only intuit that our intuition is better.

We're all lousy at intuition, and wonderful at lying to ourselves about it. The honest truth is that computers are far better at intuition than we are, because in order to know what feels "off" you have to know what's "on." In order to do that you have to constantly reassess the average of everything, then re-rank your own experience against it.

Test your own, by comparing these three anonymous lines:

Player	G	HR	AVG	OBP	SLG
Player A	156	38	.259	.342	.535
Player B	154	38	.280	.348	.527
Player C	158	38	.266	.343	.509

Miami Marlins 2019

These all seem like pretty similar players, right? The second one a touch more batted-ball dependent, the third a little less strong, but all pretty good hitters. And you'd be right, about the latter. Not the former.

Here's the breakdown:

- Player A: 1991 Howard Johnson, 141 DRC+
- Player B: 1996 Dean Palmer, 121 DRC+
- Player C: 2018 Giancarlo Stanton, 114 DRC+

Baseball is fortunate to have escaped the seismic shifts of so many other sports, where the talents and performances of other eras are nearly unrecognizable. (And not just other sports: try to explain the greatness of the movie Duck Soup without adjusting for era.) But they're still there, and they're nearly impossible to account for manually, without having to resort to sweeping generalizations like "steroid era" or "juiced-ball era" to throw out entire swathes of production.

This is all to say that we should celebrate the index stat, that simple 100-based scale with such a humble aim: just to give context. It's hard to imagine how we lived without them for so long. Sabermetricians have always tried to make their stats look like other stats: True Average mapped to batting average, FIP molded to look like and compare to ERA. It's easy to understand the motivation—these statistics carry an emotional value in them that is hard to resist, as with the .300 hitter and the 2.00 ERA—but even they fall prey to the same loss of scale as their unadjusted counterparts. If a .300 average means different things in different years, does that hold true for a .300 True Average?

Instead, 100 doesn't say anything, except above average or below. And it does it instantly, for every season in every run environment for any statistic we want it to. We should have more index stats: K%+, so we can stop comparing Mike Clevinger's career 9.46 K/9 to Nolan Ryan's 9.55. HBP%+, so we can note that Ron Hunt was getting plunked when nobody else was getting plunked, as opposed to that imitator Brandon Guyer. Some might note how stale these references are and accuse league-adjustment as a backward-looking drive, and this is true. But we're always looking backward, always comparing the new with the expectations already set. The index stat just forces us to be honest.

There's always resistance to a new statistic, especially one so outwardly simple and so internally complex. We tend to stick with what we know, even in the case of formulas that are supposed to tell us what we know. But if your resistance is that it seems too complicated, too counterintuitive, too "black boxy," I encourage you to consider why you feel that way. Because the real world is infinitely more complicated than baseball, where all the pitches go in one basic direction and the baserunners are only allowed to travel in four directions. Baseball statistics based on mixed methodology are almost impossibly intricate. So are skyscrapers and automobiles. That's why we have computers—to take the guesswork out of them.

—*Patrick Dubuque is an author of Baseball Prospectus.*

Index of Names

Alcantara, Sandy 44, 98
Alfaro, Jorge 22
Alvarez, Pedro 93
Anderson, Brian 24
Banfield, Will 68, 105
Brice, Austin 46
Brigham, Jeff 94
Brigman, Bryson 105
Brinson, Lewis 26
Cabrera, Edward 81
Castro, Starlin 28
Chen, Wei-Yin 48
Conley, Adam 50
Cooper, Garrett 69
Dean, Austin 30
Devers, Jose 70, 106
Diaz, Isan 71, 99
Dugger, Robert 82
Dunand, Joe 72, 106
Eveld, Tommy 83
Ferrell, Riley 84
Gallen, Zac 85, 101
Galloway, Isaac 32
Garcia, Jarlin 52
Garrett, Braxton 86, 103
Granderson, Curtis 34
Graves, Brett 94
Guerrero, Gabriel 93
Guerrero, Tayron 54
Guzman, Jorge 87, 102
Harrison, Monte 73, 98
Hernandez, Elieser 94
Herrera, Rosell 93
Holaday, Bryan 93
Johnson, Osiris 74
Kinley, Tyler 94
Kolek, Tyler 88
Lopez, Pablo 94
Machado, Dixon 93
Marrero, Deven 93
Mesa, Victor 107
Mesa, Victor Victor 75, 97
Meyer, Ben 94
Miller, Brian 76, 104
Neidert, Nick 89, 100
O'Brien, Peter 93
Pompey, Tristan 77, 106
Prado, Martin 36
Ramirez, Harold 78
Richards, Trevor 56
Riddle, JT 79
Rivera, Yadiel 93
Rogers, Trevor 90, 104
Rojas, Miguel 38
Romo, Sergio 58
Sanchez, Sixto 91
Scott, Connor 80, 101
Sierra, Magneuris 40
Smith, Caleb 60
Steckenrider, Drew 62
Straily, Dan 64
Urena, Jose 66

Miami Marlins 2019

Walker, Neil 42
Wallach, Chad 93
Yamamoto, Jordan 92, 103

Ballpark diagrams for Baseball Prospectus are created by THIRTY81Project, a design concept offering original ballpark artwork, including the new 'Ballparks of 2019' 11 x 17 color print.

Visit **www.thirty81project.com** for full details.

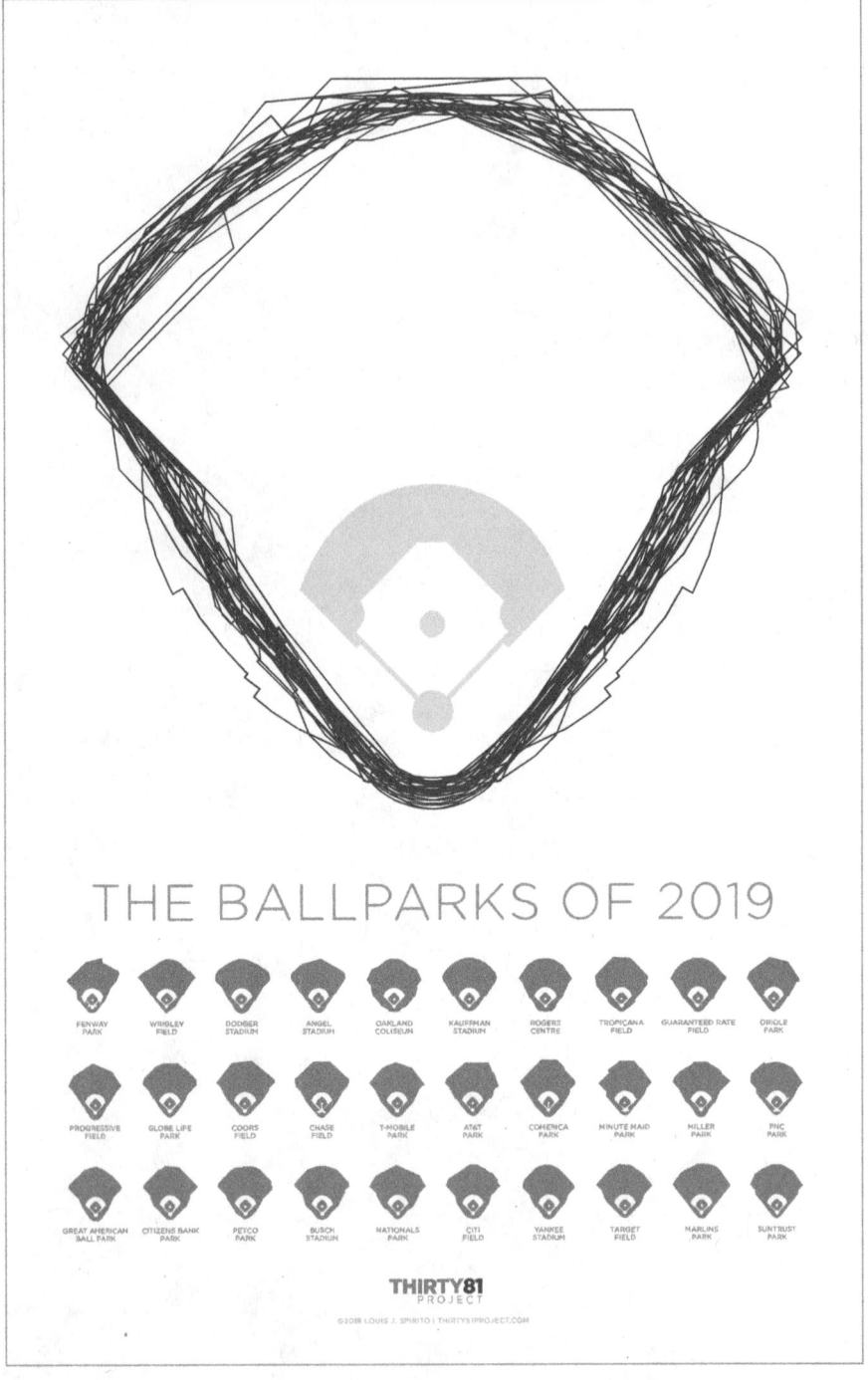